Managing Primary Classroom

SCHOOL LEADERSHIP AND MANAGEMENT SERIES

Series Editors: Brent Davies and John West-Burnham

Effective Learning in Schools
by Christopher Bowring-Carr and John West-Burnham

Managing Quality in Schools
by John West-Burnham

Reengineering and Total Quality in Schools
by Brent Davies and John West-Burnham

Middle Management in Schools
by Sonia Blandford

Resource Management in Schools
by Sonia Blandford

Strategic Marketing for Schools
by Brent Davies and Linda Ellison

Forthcoming titles:

Human Resource Management for Effective Schools
by John O'Neill and John West-Burnham

Management Development
by John West-Burnham

Strategic Development Planning in Schools
by Brent Davies and Linda Ellison

Managing Primary Classrooms

■ ■ ■

Edited by
IAN CRAIG

London · Hong Kong · Johannesburg · Melbourne · Singapore · Washington DC

PITMAN PUBLISHING
128 Long Acre, London WC2E 9AN
Tel: +44 (0) 171 447 2000
Fax: +44 (0) 171 240 5771

A Division of Pearson Professional Limited

First published in Great Britain in 1997

ISBN 0 273 62712 0

British Library Cataloguing in Publication Data
A CIP catalogue record for this book can be obtained from the British Library

10 9 8 7 6 5 4 3 2 1

Typeset by Phoenix Photosetting, Chatham, Kent
Printed and bound in Great Britain by Redwood Books, Trowbridge, Wiltshire

The Publishers' policy is to use paper manufactured from sustainable forests.

Contents

■   ■   ■

Acknowledgements

■ ■ ■

We are grateful to the following for permission to reproduce copyright material:

Routledge Publishers for Figure 2.1 from Dean, J. (1992) *Organising Learning in the Primary Classroom*; The Schools Curriculum and Assessment Authority for the original from which Figure 3.1 was adapted, from SCAA (1995) *Planning the Curriculum at Key Stages 1 and 2*; the Advisory and Inspection Division, Nottinghamshire County Council for Figure 3.2 from Nottinghamshire LEA (1994) *Developing Children's Skills in Review, Self Assessment and Target Setting*; Kent County Council Education Department for the original from which Figure 10.5 was adapted, from KCC (1996) *Aspects of Classroom Management*; and the Crown Copyright Unit for permission to reproduce quotations from HMSO publications in chapters 1, 3, 4, 5 and 11. Crown copyright is reproduced with the permission of the Controller of Her Majesty's Stationery Office.

Contributors

■ ■ ■

Mike Aylen was closely involved in planning and contributing to management development courses for teachers and headteachers during his fourteen years of headship in two contrasting Kent primary schools. As Kent LEA's Senior Primary Adviser/Inspector and an OFSTED registered inspector he is now responsible for an extensive LEA primary school review programme.

Tom Banks is Assessment Co-ordinator for Devon LEA, covering Key Stages 1–4. In a previous existence he worked in schools for fifteen years and acted as Chief Moderator for GCSE English. A member of the notorious 1980s SEAC English Committee, some famous people in education are said to have opinions about him.

David Bell is the Chief Education Officer with Newcastle City Council. He has been a primary school headteacher in Essex and an OFSTED registered inspector. In 1993/4 he was a Harkness Fellow, based in Atlanta, Georgia. Currently he is a governor of Newcastle College and a Board member of Tyneside Careers.

Julie Briant is a senior inspector with responsibility for the Early Years in Croydon. She is an OFSTED registered primary inspector, a registered nursery education inspector, and an OFSTED accredited trainer for primary and nursery inspectors. She was previously the headteacher of a nursery school and an infant school in Croydon.

Rose Collinson is a Senior Area Adviser in Kent, having previously been the County's senior consultant for assessment, working with primary, secondary and special schools. Prior to that she worked as a special needs teacher and advisory teacher in a number of London boroughs.

Ian Craig was previously the headteacher of two primary schools, a primary inspector, and the head of Kent's Curriculum Services Agency. He is now an Assistant Director of Education in Kent and an OFSTED registered inspector. He has written for many educational journals and has edited three previous books on primary school management.

Martin Garwood works for the Kent Curriculum Services Agency as a School Development Consultant. His main role is to provide advice and support to Kent's primary schools. He is an OFSTED registered inspector and was previously the headteacher of a primary school in Kent.

Penny Hickman is Project Development Officer for the Devon LEA Assessment Unit, co-ordinating the Devon School Improvement Project. She has been seconded from a large Devon primary school where she was Key Stage 1 co-ordinator. Previously she taught in a number of Leicestershire primary schools.

Maureen Hughes is currently Literary Consultant to Newcastle upon Tyne LEA on secondment from her post as headteacher of a primary school. She is also a visiting lecturer at the University of Newcastle upon Tyne. Maureen has conducted research and published papers on the relationship between children's language and thought.

John Keys is the headteacher of a large primary school in Kent, and was previously a headteacher in three other contrasting primary schools. He has lectured on primary education in Africa, Asia and the USA. He has recently been awarded an EU grant to develop science and information technology across borders.

Colleen McLaughlin is a tutor at the University of Cambridge Institute of Education, where she works on in-service education with teachers. She was previously a teacher and an advisory teacher.

RoseAnne Simpson is Principal Inspector for the London Borough of Croydon, and an OFSTED registered inspector. She was previously headteacher of an infant school in Southwark and a primary school in Lewisham. She has a strong interest in teacher development and has tutored on Early Childhood and MA Curriculum courses at Goldsmiths College.

Paul Smith has worked for the last five years as an Assessment Development Officer for Devon LEA. Before this he was the deputy headteacher of a primary school in Torquay. His previous experiences include working as an education liaison officer between the LEA and a local BBC radio station.

Laurie Thomas is a Kent Schools Adviser and past County Co-ordinator for PSHE. He has twenty years practical experience of teaching pupils with emotional and behavioural difficulties within primary, secondary and special schools. He has been a headteacher and has trained and supported teachers in this country, North America and Russia.

Introduction

■ ■ ■

'Management' is a term that we readily associate with heads and other senior teachers in schools, but very seldom with classroom teachers. However, the classroom is just a microcosm of the school and a very complex management structure in its own right. The class teacher is responsible for the day-to-day management of a very complex organisation, and of increasingly complex resources.

Primary school teachers daily manage the work and social interaction of large groups of children. They are now expected to take on leadership of other adults within the classroom, both volunteers and paid helpers, and leadership of the whole staff group in particular aspects of school life. Even inexperienced teachers are now regularly given accountabilities for large budgets. They are expected to understand state-of-the-art technology, and like any other manager in any organisation, they are expected to plan, review and be accountable for all that they do. No teacher can survive without being an expert in time management.

It is the view of many in education, and particularly of the contributors to this book, that 'management training' should begin at the classroom level.

In this book, a number of writers who still have their 'feet on the ground' in primary schools have tried to address a number of management issues that relate to classroom teachers. In using the team of writers that we do in this book, all of whom are experienced primary school educators, many of them practising or ex-heads, the book is more well informed than is often the case in books of this kind by the realities of the 'chalk-face'. In this book there should be no 'credibility gap' often found between writers and readers of books for primary teachers.

The pattern of this book is simple. In the first chapter, David Bell sets out the changing pressures on primary school teachers. In Chapters 2 to 10 various writers, all of them experienced primary teachers and advisers, deal with specific classroom issues.

In Chapters 2 and 3 RoseAnne Simpson and Rose Collinson focus on planning and assessment. In Chapters 4 and 5 Paul Smith and Laurie Thomas address the issues of managing the pupils themselves, in Chapters 6 and 7 Julie Briant and John Keys look at the general resources available in the classroom and school, and in Chapters 8 and 9 Maureen Hughes, Tom Banks and Penny

Hickman consider the 'human' resources available to the teacher. Mike Aylen explores a particular model of classroom self-review in Chapter 10.

In Chapter 11 Martin Garwood moves out of the classroom itself and looks at the whole-school management of a curriculum area, an issue that even the most inexperienced teachers must now involve themselves in at an early stage in their professional lives. Finally, Colleen McLaughlin addresses teacher stress in Chapter 12, examining the reasons for it and how it can be dealt with by the individual, the school, and the profession as a whole.

It is usual for books on teaching to be sequential; it is usually necessary to read earlier parts of the book to understand later chapters. Although there is a pattern to this book, chapters are all self-contained and can be read in any order. No chapter is too long not to be read in one sitting, and all end with a booklist for the interested reader to follow up particularly interesting ideas.

The book is intended to inform and to change practice. Many of the chapters give practical ideas for readers to use in their own classrooms. It is not intended to be an 'academic' work, only to be used by teachers and students following courses in education, but a book to be read by all those involved in teaching in primary schools as part of their normal professional reading. It is hoped that it is of equal value to the experienced teacher and to the student teacher following a course of initial teacher training.

Throughout the book, for consistency of style, all teachers (including headteachers) are referred to as *she*, and all pupils as *he*.

I would like to dedicate this book to all those teachers in primary schools who have not sought promotion beyond the classroom – they are the unsung heroes of the teaching profession, and to all those students currently training to be primary school teachers (including my own daughter Antonia). Even with all the pressures, primary teaching is still the best job in the world!

Ian Craig

1

■ ■ ■

The Changing Pressures on Teachers

DAVID BELL

Finally, all the efforts of the teacher must be pervaded by a desire to impress upon the scholars, especially when they reach the highest class, the dignity of knowledge, the duty of each pupil to use his powers to the best advantage, and the truth that life is a serious as well as a pleasant thing.

(Board of Education, 1905)

It is tempting to assume that primary teachers have only recently become accountable for their work. Yet, as this extract from *Suggestions for the Consideration of Teachers and others concerned in the work of Public Elementary Schools* makes clear, teachers have always been subject to external exhortations and pressure. However, over the past twenty years, teachers have been subject to far greater prescription from central government. Peer-group, professional pressure has been replaced by the demands of the National Curriculum and accountability to the public through the publication of end of key stage assessment results. On top of all this, regular inspection with its central focus on the quality of teaching has put teachers under scrutiny in an unprecedented way.

An emerging profession

Primary education as it is understood today has a comparatively short history. The idea that education below the age of eleven should be designated as 'primary' was first proposed in the Hadow Report of 1926, entitled, interestingly, *The Education of the Adolescent*. Previously, the vast majority of children had been educated in elementary schools which were part of 'all-age' schools. It became national policy in 1928 but then took over fifty years to implement in full.

It is important to note that Hadow did not represent a serious consideration of the needs of children below eleven. Rather, it was written in the context of making appropriate provision for older children. However, in the years after Hadow, new buildings were provided which took account of the need for specialist accommodation in the senior classes such as laboratories and craft rooms.

From the beginnings of compulsory education until after the Second World War, teachers had a narrow focus in their work. The creation of a system of 'payment by results' in the 1860s ensured that the achievement of basic levels of literacy and numeracy remained the paramount concern although schooling was always seen to have a social control function.

Although it had little direct impact on teachers, the early years of this century saw the emergence of theories about child development, learning and early years education which were to have a profound impact on the education system and the work of teachers. Froebel, Montessori and Dewey were all thinkers whose work began to influence policy makers at the Board of Education and the training colleges. The second Hadow report of 1931 entitled *Report of the Consultative Committee on the Primary School* reflected some of these influences with its emphasis on the social and intellectual development of children. Most commentators, however, agree that its 'progressive' outlook had little impact on the practice of teachers.

The Education Act of 1944 established, in statutory terms, two stages of education, primary and secondary (although this was further complicated in the 1960s by the creation of middle schools in different parts of the country). Throughout the 1940s and 1950s, teachers were subject to new pressures as a result of the 1944 Act. The existence of a selection examination at age eleven ensured a continuing focus on literacy and numeracy as did large classes taught in small rooms. In words that could only have been written in the 1970s, given what was to come, Galton, Simon and Croll (1980) comment as follows:

> It is difficult now to reconstruct the intense pressure on schools and teachers that built up in the 1940s and 1950s relating to the selection examination; the league tables that parents drew up for local schools, the telephoning round to find out who had done well and the sense of failure that some teachers experienced when their pupils won fewer places than others, or than expected; not to speak of the effects on the children.

There was clearly a tension at the heart of primary teachers' work. On the one hand, they were increasingly influenced by 'activity' or 'discovery' methods and a greater emphasis on a child-centred approach. Yet, on the other hand, the 11-plus did impose a demand on teachers to ensure that good results were obtained, both for their pupils and the school.

Notwithstanding these pressures, teachers had significant control of their professional affairs over the preceding fifty years. In the early part of the century, teachers had demonstrated that they were a political force to be reckoned with. In fact, H.A.L. Fisher, the President of the Board of Education at the end of the First World War had suggested that a resentful teaching profession was a menace to the stability of the state. To some extent, improvements in teachers' economic position at that time reflected both a recognition that they were professionals or semi-professionals and a desire to divert them from subversive activities. As Grace (1987) points out, by the 1940s:

> ... it appeared that elementary school teachers could be given greater autonomy in schools without any serious danger to the interests of the dominant social group ensuing.

In fact, it went beyond that. There was a strong sense that teachers were 'important partners in a great education enterprise' (Grace, 1987). Significant professional autonomy had been granted to teachers, within the context of the pressures of the 11-plus. The acceptance that direct state control of teachers' work was inappropriate helped to enhance teachers' claims to professional status as did the sense of partnership that pervaded the system.

The 1960s and the 1970s: from self-determination to national crisis?

Thirty years on, it is tempting to see the 1960s in simplistic terms. One view would suggest that teachers were under no pressure at all and were able to do what they liked in the afterglow of The Plowden Report *Children and their Primary Schools* (Central Advisory Council for Education, 1967). Another view is that many teachers were subject to intolerable ideological pressure and were forced to teach in ways alien to them at the behest of progressive advisers and college lecturers. The most widely held view is that the 1960s were the beginning of the end of teacher autonomy and that they paved the way for the radical reforms of the 1980s and 1990s.

As always, the truth is more complex. It was a time of major educational change. Not only did comprehensive education take hold, the Robbins Report led to a massive expansion in higher education. Undoubtedly, the publication of The Plowden Report was a defining moment in English primary education. Although its content and impact have been debated endlessly since, it represented the spirit of the age. While difficult to quantify, the challenging of authority, increased freedom and a more relaxed view of morality would have influenced teachers and pupils alike.

Plowden undoubtedly endorsed a child-centred view of education with an emphasis on the uniqueness of each child. In operational terms, it advocated a flexible but integrated view of the curriculum with a different role for the teacher. However distorted it became in practice, one sentence in the 'Recommendations and Conclusions' of the report seemed to sum up its approach to teaching (or the lack of it!):

'Finding out' has proved to be better for children than 'being told'.

It is genuinely difficult to assess the impact all of this had on teachers. Did it reduce the pressure that had been on them in the selective system only to replace it with the new pressure of 'freedom'? Clearly, there was a tendency to experiment within schools and many headteachers were content to allow a range of teaching strategies and approaches to flourish, even within a single institution. Local education authorities expanded their advisory services and many talented and innovative individuals promoted and encouraged more flexible approaches within schools.

By the mid-1970s, there was increasing unease about the state of education. Right-wing commentators began to produce Black Papers which bemoaned the state of education (the first one in 1969 on primary education). Matters came to a head after the events in 1975 at William Tyndale Junior School in London became known. Under a headteacher who had extreme views about progressive education, the school effectively went out of control. Eventually, the Inner London Education Authority stepped in and took control of the school. A public inquiry was held in under the Chairmanship of Robin Auld QC. William Tyndale very quickly became associated with 1960s, progressive primary education. This was followed by Neville Bennett's 1976 study which appeared to condemn the informal methods of the primary school. In addition, the then Prime Minister, James Callaghan, instituted 'The Great Debate' about educational standards following a speech at Ruskin College Oxford.

Her Majesty's Inspectors were also reporting in critical terms about the standards and quality of education although, interestingly, their major report on primary education (DES, 1978), suggested that the vast majority of schools had not adopted an extreme Plowdenesque education. On the contrary, HMI criticised schools for retaining a narrowly focused curriculum. However, and this was to be portent for things to come, HMI were particularly critical of the inconsistency they found across schools in terms of curriculum coverage and planning.

The 1970s also saw an increasing focus on classroom observation as the basis of research in primary education. The most important was the ORACLE research (Observational Research and Classroom Learning Evaluation) which ran for over five years. Over time, this work developed a number of observation schedules which yielded a mass of significant information about how teachers taught. The evidence suggested that teachers were a long way from Plowden's notion of learning by discovery. Teachers were found to interact with pupils for 80 per cent of the observed time, whereas, conversely, pupils only interacted with teachers for 16 per cent of the time. What it did demonstrate, however, was the extent to which teachers individualised their instruction. For nearly 60 per cent of the day, the teacher was working with one pupil at a time. Whole-class teaching had certainly reduced in prominence although demands for it reappeared in the late 1980s and the 1990s. The research also suggested that Plowden's aspirations for pupils to work in collaborative group work had not been achieved. As one of the leading ORACLE researchers put it:

> A group simply defined the place where a pupil sat and the other pupils who sat with him.
>
> (Galton, 1987)

The radical reforms of the 1980s and 1990s

By the time the Conservative Government under Margaret Thatcher was elected in 1979, the post-war consensus in education was over. HMI began to issue a series of reports on subjects of the curriculum which laid the foundations for a national curriculum. A decisive shift came about following the effective failure of the teachers' industrial action in the mid-1980s. Teachers found their negotiating rights removed and their pay set by the School Teachers Review Body. Each year, teachers had their statutory pay and conditions spelled out in a government circular. All teachers were given greater curriculum responsi-bilities at school level and this proved to be an extremely telling pressure in small primary schools. Some teachers found themselves carrying two or three major areas of work. In addition, teachers now had to work for a contracted 1,265 hours a year. This was perceived as yet another attack on their pro-fessional status. Teachers were no longer seen as partners but as representing 'producer' interests at the expensive of the 'consumers', i.e. parents.

Beginning in 1980, the government introduced a series of reforms to give parents greater say over the choice of school for their children. But it was the Education Reform Act of 1988 which marked the decisive moment in post-war educational history. Teachers were now to be no longer trusted with the content of the curriculum. Local education authorities were to be stripped of many of their responsibilities as power was decentralised down to school level and exercised through governing bodies. The rights of parents were further strengthened by assessments that were to be made of children's progress through the National Curriculum.

The years following 1988 proved to be traumatic for many teachers as they found the pressures on them multiplied far beyond their expectations. It is hard to overstate the impact of the National Curriculum which prescribed in great detail the content of what they had to teach. Teachers found themselves having to acquire subject expertise in areas which were unfamiliar to them, such as science and technology. In addition, subjects such as history and geography expanded in range, and unfamiliar content was introduced. Few teachers were left unscathed as every curriculum co-ordinator became responsible for mapping out their school's work against the National Curriculum require-ments. Many teachers and headteachers left the profession and this was further exacerbated by the introduction of testing at the end of Key Stage 1 which was subsequently followed with testing at the end of Key Stage 2. Even in 1992, the so-called 'Three Wise Men' had to conclude:

> ... the task of the primary teacher has changed significantly with the advent of the national curriculum. Year 1 and 2 teachers, in particular have invested enormous time and energy in coming to terms with the new statutory requirements ... As we write, primary schools are teaching the statutory orders for six of the nine national curriculum subjects, will shortly be planning for the introduction of the remaining three and are preparing for the second full run of Key Stage 1 assessment.
>
> (Alexander, Rose and Woodhead, 1992)

Lawn (1988) summed up the government's changing view of teachers:

> Professionalism in the primary school has moved on from being classroom-based, usually in isolation from other teachers, fairly well defined by the head, but in the context of responsibility and autonomy, to a collective, school-wide job, based on narrowly defined through complex tasks within a context of shared management functions and tight areas of responsibility clearly defined and appraised.

All of this was a barely concealed attack on the teaching profession. As the then Chairman of the National Curriculum Council put it in his memoirs:

> The national curriculum was a deliberate attempt to put teachers in their place. They were consulted neither about its shaping nor its content.
>
> (Graham, 1996)

While all this was happening, Local Management of Schools (LMS) was being introduced. Governors became responsible for areas such as finance, buildings and personnel. The pressures on teachers were compounded as many governors were forced to make staffing reductions in the context of reducing budgets.

There was no let up in the 1990s. As Graham (1996) points out, when describing the appointment of Kenneth Clarke as Secretary of State for Education:

> Fresh from health where he had sorted out doctors and nurses, he was more than ready for teachers.

The National Curriculum then underwent two re-writes with the government eventually calling in Sir Ron Dearing to simplify the content of what was to be taught. Teachers were also having to cope with the introduction of appraisal. Although it turned out to be something of a toothless tiger in practice, its focus on classroom observation and target setting was a further pressure on teachers.

But it was the creation of the Office for Standards in Education (OFSTED) and the introduction of regular school inspection which intensified the pressure on teachers. Up until then, many teachers could go through a whole career without ever encountering an inspection. All of that changed. By the middle of 1998, every primary school in the country will have been subject to an inspection under the OFSTED arrangements. At the heart of the process is observation of teachers at work in their own classrooms. As the Inspection Schedule puts it:

Teaching is the major factor contributing to pupils' attainment, progress and response. Evaluation of the quality and impact of teaching is central to inspection.
(OFSTED, 1995)

The inspection of teachers at work is rigorous and thorough as, amongst other things, judgements about teachers are based on the extent to which they:

- set high expectations so as to challenge pupils and deepen their knowledge and understanding;
- plan effectively;
- manage pupils well and achieve high standards of discipline;
- assess pupils' work thoroughly and constructively, and use assessments to inform teaching.

(OFSTED, 1995)

On top of all of this, schools which fail to deliver an acceptable standard of education are declared as requiring special measures. By the end of 1996, over fifty primary schools were in this category.

More significantly, the debate about standards in primary schools became increasingly strident in tone. Issues about teaching and learning in primary schools had first been raised in 1992 following the report by the 'Three Wise Men'. One of them, Chris Woodhead, went on to became Her Majesty's Chief Inspector of Schools. Eschewing the discretion of his predecessors, Woodhead criticised many facets of primary education in his public, and often controversial, statements. By the mid-1990s, primary teachers felt increasingly beleaguered as attacks mounted on them following reports on the teaching of reading and the results of National Curriculum tests for 11-year-olds in English, mathematics and science. The revised inspection arrangements also allowed for the grading of teachers on a 1 to 7 scale, with a '6' or a '7' being considered poor. With a limited number of such gradings on an inspection, inspectors are duty-bound to inform the teacher concerned and their headteacher.

The research evidence supported the view that teachers were under greater pressure. Campbell *et al.* (1993) identified four particular pressures which infant teachers felt. First, poor LEA in-service training and inadequate school management wasted their time. Second, a paranoia about accountability had set in. Third, teachers saw their classrooms as less joyful places with inadequate time to follow up pupils' spontaneous interests. And finally, most teachers had lowered their career aspirations and no longer wanted promotion to headship or deputy headship.

Campbell and Neil's work (1994) was an analysis of 7,000 working days from over 700 teachers between 1990 and 1992. At a conservative estimate, the authors concluded that primary teachers were working some 400 hours a year in excess of their contracted time. Interestingly, they conclude:

> *The interviews revealed that a moral sense of obligation to do the best they could for their pupils was both a highly significant reason given by teachers for working long hours, and also seen as a cause of stress and conflict in their working lives.*

The Office of Manpower Economics' 1996 study concluded that workloads were perceived to have risen, not from a specific date but over a period of years. Primary teachers felt under particular pressure because they had limited or no non-contact time. Yet, their after-school time was increasingly taken up by management or whole-school responsibilities.

This all seems a far cry from the 1960s and the apogee of teacher autonomy. However, working in complete isolation brought its own kinds of pressures. It could be argued that teachers are now encouraged to be 'whole-school professionals'. They retain a significant amount of control over how they teach in their own classrooms. Yet, at the same time, development planning at the school level has allowed them to make a more purposeful contribution to the management at the school. Continuity and progression, buzzwords of the 1990s, are important as they provide pupils with a more consistent experience throughout their time in primary school. Equally, they ensure that teachers plan and work together.

Primary teachers have also become more sophisticated in their use of evidence to refine professional judgement. Good primary teachers have always had an initiative 'feel' for the progress being made by pupils. Sophisticated use of assessment techniques has brought more rigour to this process. Hargreaves and Hopkins (1991) talk about making 'considered professional judgements' which can then be refined through discussion with others, establishing agreement on standards, engaging in mutual observation in classrooms and using informed external opinion.

Clearly teachers need expert professional development to contribute effectively. Again, this has changed over time with teachers' needs being put into a whole-school context to ensure that individual needs are consistent with institutional needs. It is, however, important to say something about class size as this has become something of a touchstone for teachers under pressure. The 1996 workload study by the Office of Manpower Economics is quite unequivocal:

> *Class size affected workload. The increase tended to be not only in terms of the number of pupils taught but also related to a greater range of ability. Time spent with individual pupils often spilled over into breaktimes or lunch. There was likely to be some more planning, preparation, reporting, profiling, recording and disciplinary load which increased stress and the consequent need for recovery time.*

In 1996, between a quarter and a third of all primary pupils were taught in classes with over 30 pupils. Undoubtedly, this masks the extent to which non-teaching staff are being used to improve adult–child ratios. However, as the above quotation makes clear, the issue of class size is not simply a question of numbers. It relates to increasing demand on teachers' time both inside and outside the classroom. The assessment of individual pupils' work has also increased and this is largely a task which remains with the teacher irrespective of other adults in the classroom.

The controversy over class size has been exacerbated by a bitter debate over whether or not it makes any difference to pupil attainment. There is surprisingly little British research on this subject although what there is, coupled with international work, tends to suggest that smaller classes are more important in the early years of primary education. A number of research projects are now under way to examine this subject in some detail, although by its very nature, such work is unlikely to yield significant results in the short term.

Schoolhouse or prisonhouse?

So far the focus has been on the external pressures which face teachers. As has been demonstrated, these have changed and intensified over time. However, it is worth reflecting on the pressures which are inherent in being a primary school teacher, irrespective of outside influences.

In terms of basic organisation, primary schools have changed remarkably little over this century. The vast majority of primary teachers teach the same class of children for the majority of the time. Despite the National Curriculum and increasing demands for subject specialisation at the end of Key Stage 2, very few schools have experimented with a secondary model of organisation. Primary schools are relatively small organisations. The average size of a primary school in England is 224. The teaching force is 80 per cent female although headships are disproportionately held by men.

Comparatively little was written about the organisational dynamics of schools until the 1970s. In 1979, Rutter *et al.* published a seminal piece of research which looked in great detail at the organisational life and culture of secondary schools. This was followed by a similar project in junior schools (Mortimore *et al.*, 1988), which identified the characteristics of effective schools.

The work of Nias and latterly Southworth and Nias has proved to be influential in providing an understanding of what actually happens in primary schools and to primary teachers in the course of their day-to-day work:

> *For a number of historical, philosophical, psychological and cultural reasons, teachers in English primary schools are socialised (from their pre-service education*

9

onwards) into a tradition of isolation, individualism, self-reliance and authority – in which high value is attached to self-investment and the establishment of a personal relationship with pupils.

(Nias, 1989)

Primary teaching makes heavy emotional and personal demands on individuals. In a sense, their problems are compounded by their acceptance of a wide range of responsibilities for their pupils, well beyond the narrowly educational. A number of writers have commented on the extent to which primary teachers have to reflect continually at their practice even though they have little time to do so. In practice, teachers have to reconcile a number of tensions within their work. Moyles (1992) identified ten such tensions including:

- dealing with individuals, yet working towards meeting all children's basic educational needs;

- supporting children, yet not allowing the development of unnecessary and inappropriate dependency;

- having conviction about what one is doing, yet being flexible enough to acknowledge that which requires reappraisal.

An even more radical analysis comes from Steedman (1987) who takes a feminist perspective. She characterises the primary teacher as the 'mother made conscious'. She also highlights the significant emotional bonds which exist between children and teachers. Ultimately, she concludes:

Teaching young children must always be in some way or another, a retreat from general social life and from fully adult relationships, a way of becoming Lucy Snowe's dormouse, rolled up in the prisonhouse, the school house.

All of this may be seen as an exaggeration. Worse still, it could be argued that this is a sociological construct of reality which bears little relation to how primary teachers see their work. However, the evidence does suggest that primary teachers still see themselves as working in relative isolation from their professional colleagues. In addition, there is little dispute over the emotional pressure that primary teachers feel in their jobs. Nias (1988) captures a vivid comment from one teacher about how she sees her job:

You don't actually go into teaching unless you're a caring person. And the thing about caring is that you care twenty-four hours a day, you don't just care from nine till half past three and so you take your worries, your thoughts with you, you take your enthusiasms home with you. I mean when I leave here I'll go and walk around the town and I'll have half an eye open on what I might be doing on Monday.

There is a danger of overstating the negative characteristics of being a primary teacher. Although the job is undoubtedly more stressful than it was, teachers still find enormous satisfaction in working with children. Teachers will often highlight the satisfaction they derive from seeing children learn, they will also highlight many other rewards of being with children such as sharing ideas, helping them become increasingly independent and supporting them in times of difficulty.

Although she was writing in the late 1980s, Nias (1989) found that teachers' job satisfaction did not wane over time:

> Successful and committed mid-career teachers appear to find their work extremely satisfying, deriving from it a strong sense of fit between self and occupation, and a good deal of self-esteem.

Towards the twenty-first century

It is fair to say that primary teachers are under greater pressure now than they have ever been. As individuals, they carry major subject co-ordination responsibilities alongside their basic classroom teaching responsibility. They are under significant scrutiny through the appraisal process and their work as classroom teachers is subject to the rigours of regular external inspection. As part of a team of teachers working in a school, the performance of their pupils is now monitored in an unprecedented way and reported on publicly through the publication of end of key stage assessments. In addition, throughout the 1990s, they have been subject to critical comments from politicians, educational experts and the media. This paper has also identified the inherent pressures in dealing with young children and being, to some extent, detached from the adult working world. On top of all that as Delamont (1987) has argued:

> There is a powerful rhetoric of abuse levelled at primary teachers which has little relation to facts or evidence and is remarkably resistant to rational argument.

Yet, for all of that, the picture looks cautiously optimistic. There does appear to be a period of calm ahead with major changes to the curriculum ruled out until at least the turn of the century. Teachers seem much more comfortable with the rigour of the national curriculum and the undoubted benefits it has brought in terms of subject co-ordination and whole school planning. National initiatives such as literacy and numeracy centres seem designed to build consensus around the 'how' of teaching as well as the 'what'. Professional development is given a far greater status than it has ever been given in the past. For all the pressures, young people still come forward in droves to train as primary teachers. Why? The last word should be with a primary teacher:

> 'It's what is called the three cherries syndrome: where you can work with a child for weeks and weeks and weeks and you feel you're achieving nothing. And then one morning there's a look in their eye which just tells you 'I understand now!' and it's as if the three cherries have arrived on the slot machine.

> (Nias, 1989)

11

References

Alexander, R., Rose, J. and Woodhead, C. (1992), *Curriculum Organisation and Classroom Practice in Primary Schools*, Department of Education and Science.

Bennett, N. (1976), *Teaching Styles and Pupil Progress*, Open Books.

Board of Education (1905), *Suggestions for the Consideration of Teachers and others concerned in the work of Public Elementary Schools*, HMSO.

Campbell, J., Evans, L., Neil, S. and Packwood, A. (1993), 'The National Curriculum and the Management of Infant Teachers Time', in Preedy, M. (ed.), *Managing the Effective School*, Paul Chapman Publishing.

Campbell, R.J. and Neill, S.R. (1994), *Primary Teachers at Work*, Routledge.

Central Advisory Council for Education (1967), *Children and their Primary Schools*, HMSO.

Delamont, S. (1987), 'The Primary Teacher 1945–1990: Myths and Realities', in Delamont, S. (ed.), *The Primary School Teacher*, Falmer.

Department of Education and Science (1978), *Primary Education in England*, HMSO.

Galton, M. (1987), 'An Oracle Chronicle: A Decade of Classroom Research', in Delamont, S. (ed.), *The Primary School Teacher*, Falmer.

Galton, M., Simon, B. and Croll, P. (1980), *Inside the Primary Classroom*, Routledge and Kegan Paul.

Grace, G. (1987), 'Teachers and the State in Britain: A Changing Relation', in Lawn, M. and Grace, G. (eds), *Teachers: The Culture and Politics of Work*, Falmer.

Graham, D. (1996), *The Education Racket*, Neil Wilson Publishing.

Hargreaves, D. and Hopkins, D. (1991), *The Empowered School*, Cassell.

Lawn, M. (1988), 'Skill in Schoolwork: Work Relations in the Primary School', in Ozga, J. (ed.), *Schoolwork*, Open University Press.

Mortimore, P., Sammons, P., Stoll, L., Lewis, D. and Ecob, R. (1988), *School Matters*, Open Books.

Moyles, J. (1992), *Organising for Learning in the Primary Classroom*, Open University Press.

Nias, J. (1988), 'What it Means to Feel Like a Teacher: The Subjective Reality of Primary School Teaching', in Ozga, J. (ed.), *Schoolwork*, Open University Press.

Nias, J. (1989), *Primary Teachers Talking*, Routledge.

Office of Manpower Economics on behalf of the School Teachers' Review Body (1996), *Managing Teachers' Workloads*, Social and Community Planning Research Council.

OFSTED (1995), *Guidance on the Inspection of Nursery and Primary Schools*, HMSO.

Rutter, M., Maughan, B., Mortimore, P. and Ouston, J. (1979), *Fifteen Thousand Hours*, Open Books.

Steedman, C. (1987), 'Prisonhouses', in Lawn, M. and Grace, G. (eds), *Teachers: The Culture and Politics of Work*, Falmer.

2

■ ■ ■

Planning for Learning

ROSEANNE SIMPSON

Planning the work they give to children is not new for primary teachers. To a greater or lesser extent they have always planned what they do in the classroom, and many have done it very successfully. For many teachers their planning allowed them to experiment with their creativity and skill in the art of teaching. In the past classrooms reflected the individual style and expertise of the teacher, often with little reference to the work being done in other classrooms in the same school. Whereas talented and inspirational teachers blossomed in this climate of individuality, those teachers who were weak, ill-prepared or simply uninspired remained largely undisturbed by external influences. Consequently, pupils' access to the systematic and continuous development of skills, knowledge and understanding was entirely dependent upon which series of teachers they had during their primary schooling.

The introduction (1988) and revision (1995) of the National Curriculum and its assessment have caused major changes in the ways in which teaching and learning are organised in primary classrooms, requiring more detailed and thorough planning than ever before. The impact of OFSTED inspections, and the use of the OFSTED Framework by local education authority (LEA) inspectors and by schools themselves in reviewing their own work, have reinforced and further developed this expectation. National and international work on school improvement has also made a major contribution to the widening and deepening debate about what makes good schools, effective teaching and successful learners. Significant factors which influence quality include clear leadership, particularly of the curriculum, consistency among teachers, and intellectually challenging teaching (Mortimore et al., 1988).

What is very clear now is that teachers can no longer be entirely autonomous in terms of what they teach and how. Co-operation and collaboration among teachers are at the heart of successful teaching and learning, leading to consistency when working towards common aims, establishing common

13

principles of procedure and practice and, crucially, using common forms of planning and assessment. The success of a class teacher's planning is consequently dependent upon the quality of whole school planning, including the effectiveness with which the school has mapped out the systematic, year by year, coverage of all subjects of the National Curriculum, religious education, and provision for pupils' personal and social development.

It is in the ways in which she interprets the school's planned curriculum for her pupils that today's class teacher must continue to develop the skills, expertise and creativity which makes her an individual, thinking professional, prepared to try new ideas and take risks, not allowing her inspiration to be stifled, but letting it breath, develop and inspire others.

The whole curriculum

There is now useful guidance for primary schools when planning the whole curriculum (SCAA, 1995; Proctor *et al.*, 1995). Detailed advice on the important features of whole school planning cover three broad levels, each having its own function and purpose. These are **long, medium**, and **short-term planning**.

Long-term planning focuses on producing a broad curriculum framework for each year of the key stage. SCAA recommend that this reflects the school's overall curricular aims and should involve all staff and governors at different stages of the process. The school is encouraged to match the different elements of the curriculum with the available time for teaching. Other planning issues are coverage of the full statutory curriculum; *progression* in all subjects of the curriculum; *balance* within and between subjects; *coherence* within and between subjects; and *continuity* between year groups and key stages.

Medium-term planning covers the detail of what is to be taught to each year group, and opportunities for its assessment. SCAA recommend that this involves year group or key stage teachers, supported by co-ordinators. Cross-curricular elements, such as considerations of equal opportunities and ways of developing pupils' spiritual, moral, social and cultural experiences should be included at this stage of planning. Diagrams or tables which set out the work to be covered in any one unit at this stage are necessarily comprehensive, as they need to take account of the appropriate subject content, as well as other considerations such as the context of learning for the pupils. If key aspects of learning are not included in the planning at this point there is a danger that they will be overlooked at the point of teaching.

Short-term planning is what class teachers do from week to week and from day to day, and is what this chapter will explore in more depth.

Organising planning for learning

Much of the long and medium-term planning described above deals with the content of the curriculum and what is to be 'covered'. When this comes down to the reality of the teacher's day-to-day planning a much more important question for her to ask is: *What do I want these children to learn?*

Using the units of work allocated to her year group, the class teacher sets about ordering them into weekly or bi-weekly blocks, planning to teach the required skills, concepts and knowledge according to her assessment of what the pupils are ready to learn. The teacher then needs to make a number of important decisions, such as how she will organise the material for teaching and the pupils for learning, the teaching style she will use, her use of language, the questions she will ask of which pupils, and how she might assess what the children have learned.

Joan Dean (1983; 1992) suggests a sequence for planning which can be used as a checklist or planning chart. It assumes that much work in primary classrooms is done through topics, while acknowledging that the need to ensure progression within the subjects of the curriculum has prompted many primary teachers to limit the range of the topic within one or perhaps two subject areas. The main features of this model, illustrated in Figure 2.1, take the teacher through a series of considerations within a common format, each time she sets about planning a lesson or activity:

- Begin by identifying pupils' *existing experience* within the topic to establish: What do they already understand?
- Decide what direct, or *first-hand experience* can be arranged to enhance the quality of what is to be taught and give it meaning.
- Decide what *language* the children need to understand to do this work; which words and phrases, specific vocabulary; what *new language* do they need?
- *Knowledge* – What does she want them to *know* when they have finished?
- *Concepts* – What does she want them to *understand*?
- *Skills* – What does she want them to be able to *do* as a result of this piece of work.
- What opportunities are there for pupils to develop their learning through *creative work*, for example art, textiles, music, expressive language? (An additional consideration here could be possible opportunities to develop pupils' spiritual, moral, social and cultural understanding.)
- *Outcomes* – How will they show the teacher what they have learned.

This planning format gives a clear picture of what the teacher expects the children to learn, without inhibiting other possibilities which may emerge.

Existing experience	Experience of a variety of materials in everyday life – fabric, food, furniture materials, building materials, use of yarn in clothing, knitting, woodwork, experience with clay, etc.	
First-hand experience	Visit local street and small manufacturing unit, e.g. a pottery; bring in fabrics; dig clay; collect sheep's wool; collect similar sized twigs of different woods; survey buildings; visit building site	
Language	Names of different fabrics, dye plants, stones, woods, etc. Transparent, opaque, porous, inflammable, saturated, flexible, rigid, man-made material, natural material Discussion of how to test materials; presentation to others of findings; use of books to find out; writing of reports of findings	
Knowledge	Sources of different materials; their characteristics; uses of different materials	
Concepts	Some materials are natural and some are man-made; different materials have different characteristics which determine their use	
Skills	Testing materials for different characteristics, e.g. hardness/softness, flexibility, etc.; making bricks and pots; making dyes; spinning; weaving	
Creative work	Making a picture with stones; making bricks and pottery; making dyes and using them; making a fabric collage; spinning and weaving; writing about how different materials make you feel	
Outcomes	Exhibition of work; discussion of experiments and findings; planning for presentation to parents	

Figure 2.1: Short-term planning model
(*Source*: From Dean, 1992)

Planning for successful teaching

There is substantial evidence emerging, for example from OFSTED inspections (1996), that teaching is more effective when teachers are clear about the objectives for the lesson and when these are shared with the pupils. Evaluation of the inspections carried out in 1994/5 showed that in two out of three schools at Key Stage 1 and half the schools at Key Stage 2 lessons were generally well planned and had clear objectives. The most successful planning used a range of teaching methods to ensure that pupils were suitably challenged and that they made effective progress in the time available. The majority of good lessons consisted of a blend of direct teaching to the whole class, to groups or individuals so that teaching closely matched their existing attainment and built upon it.

These findings confirm what many teachers have known about good teaching for some time. When a pupil understands, for example, that he needs to know about tens and units and be able to add and subtract them in order to know how much money he needs to buy his favourite game in the real world, he is better disposed to learning than when faced simply with sets of confusing numbers. The teacher who keeps pupils informed and involved in the purpose of their learning is more likely to sustain their motivation, interest and determination to succeed.

Teaching style

Much has been written about the teaching methods used in primary classrooms in recent years. There have been many contradictory arguments about the relative strengths and weaknesses of teaching the whole class, teaching groups of pupils, or teaching individuals (Alexander, 1992; OFSTED: Annual Reports of HMCI, 1992/3; 1993/4). Like many arguments in education these have often been over-simplified, expressed in an unhelpful, polarised manner which serves only to deflect sensible and rational debate. OFSTED's findings (1996 op. cit.) that the most successful teaching uses a blend of methods is significant in that it confirms fairly conclusively that no single teaching style, used exclusively, can fully meet the requirements of the curriculum or the needs of pupils.

Teachers must choose the teaching style most suited to the material they wish to teach, the pupils and their particular learning needs, the resources required and the time available for teaching. It is often a more economical use of time, for example, to introduce a new topic to the whole class, covering broad principles and explaining the sequence of activities and their purpose, than to cover this level of generality within small teaching groups. Work with pupils in small groups is often better suited to extending or reinforcing the concepts to be learned according to the ability of the pupils.

For example most Year 5 pupils should know how simple circuits work in electricity and how switches can be used to control, say, the lights in a model house. The class teacher wishes to introduce further developments of this work, including the use of series and parallel circuits. The first part of the lesson might involve the whole class, reviewing with the teacher what they already know about simple circuits. This may involve discussion about the use of circuits in everyday electrical devices. The teacher would use the opportunity to demonstrate the next stage of the process, introducing the notion of the need for more complex circuits in certain situations, such as in traffic signals or in the lighting system at home. The teacher would encourage pupils to make hypotheses, based on their existing knowledge. Depending on the resources available the teacher might then organise the pupils to work in groups, to experiment with the materials, make and record their own parallel or series circuits. Assessment of the pupils' progress in this activity may then prompt the teacher to draw together a few of the more able pupils to develop their circuits into working models with a particular purpose, for example devising an anti-burglar timed switch to operate the lights in the house at appropriate intervals. A few pupils may require further individual attention, to challenge those who are particularly able or to support the slow learner. The class teacher must always exercise her professional judgement about the most appropriate means of ensuring that the purpose of the lesson, based on her knowledge of the pupils, is fulfilled. A prerequisite of this is careful and detailed planning.

Pace and challenge

A significant feature of good teaching is the pace at which lessons are taught; this is linked with teachers' expectations of what pupils are capable of achieving. In recent years the evidence from Reading Recovery teaching which takes place in some areas of this country as well as in New Zealand, has shown the extent to which individual pupils can make significant progress in reading and in their levels of confidence by the high teacher expectations and fast pace of the lessons (Marie Clay, 1993; University of London, Institute of Education, 1996). Children who have been diagnosed as the slowest readers in their class, and are therefore already failing as learners at the tender age of six years, are put under pressure in daily, highly demanding half-hour sessions, where their carefully diagnosed learning needs are met with the skill and expertise of the trained Reading Recovery teacher. The great majority of these children respond with evident enjoyment, growing enthusiasm and confidence to the fast pace and high expectations of these lessons; on return to their classes these pupils can often cope with their class work as well as or better than their classmates, (almost 80 per cent were successful in the programme during 1995/6). This shows us that children are capable of working at challenging levels and a brisk pace, as long as the work and the teaching are well matched to their learning needs.

Matching planning to what pupils are expected to learn

The class teacher's task is to get the match of pace, challenge and level of content as close as possible to the extension of children's capabilities. Planning grids which are increasingly being used in classrooms across the country have gone through many different formats in teachers' attempts to get this aspect of their planning right. Early models started with the activities the teacher would provide, such as 'planting cress seeds; observing and measuring the rate of growth' for example. All pupils would do the activity in rotating groups. The teacher's evaluation would often focus on the success of the practical activity, rather than what the children had learned or understood about what plants need to grow. Teachers are becoming increasingly aware of the need to begin, not from the activity, but from the learning they intend to take place. A planning grid to help this process might look something like that in Figure 2.2 for a Year 2 class studying 'Life Processes and Living Things' in science:

This level of planning, of course, must be based on the teacher's knowledge of the subject and of the children, the pupils' levels of understanding, their existing experience of what is to be learned, and their particular learning needs, for example in literacy and numeracy. The teacher might expect mathematically able pupils to measure the rate of growth in standard units using a metric ruler, whereas pupils who had not yet reached that stage might still need to use non-standard units such as unifix cubes. The teacher must also be careful to provide pupils with reading and writing tasks which they can cope with, so that underdeveloped literacy skills do not deter children's learning in science. Similarly, able readers and writers should be encouraged to work at more demanding levels, for example they might use information books to find out more about the topic, and explain what they have learned in writing. The teacher should make extensive use of talk and discussion throughout the work with all pupils, to develop their understanding, skills and knowledge in the aspects of learning identified in the 'learning' column, at levels to suit pupils' ability.

Knowing the children: assessment

We know that classroom assessment is a skilled and complex process which many teachers find difficult to record, particularly in terms of perceived National Curriculum requirements. However if we return to the simplest of principles about what makes good teaching the complications which have arisen over National Curriculum Assessment can be placed in context. Mary Jane Drummond (1993) reminds us that:

> When we work with children, when we play and experiment and talk with them, when we watch them and everything they do, we are witnessing a fascinating and inspiring process; we are seeing them learn. As we think about what we see, and try to understand it, we have embarked upon the process that ... I am calling assessment.

She uses the term to describe what teachers do as part of their everyday practice. That is to say they are involved in the skills of observation and reflection, part of what should be the basic and fundamental expertise of the teacher. Drummond goes on to describe how this assessment can help teachers to appreciate and understand pupils' achievements, their individuality, and consequently the differences between them. It can be used to shape and enrich the curriculum, can determine the ways in which teachers talk with and listen

What will the children learn?	How shall I organise them?	What shall I do – direct teaching?	What will the children do?	Resources needed	How shall I assess what they know and understand?
1. That plants need light and water to grow 2. To develop the notion of testing to find out 3. To develop skills of: observing explaining hypothesising measuring recording	Whole class	1. Use children's experience of plants in the class or in the park to talk about what helps them to grow. 2. Ask questions to encourage children to hypothesise about what might happen in different conditions. 3. Encourage them to suggest how they might find out for themselves, using cress seeds, for example. 4. Teach specific vocabulary and use it in context, e.g. seeds, soil, root, stem. Encourage children to use correct terms in discussion. 5. Plan 'extending' questions to ask the more able in discussion.	Listen, answer questions; talk about what they know. Hypothesise; suggest ways of finding out.	Plants, flowers growing in the classroom, school garden or park; pictures of these if the real experience is not possible.	Note children's responses to questions; ask further questions of increasing complexity as children demonstrate understanding. How closely do children observe detail; do they ask questions; can they explain what they have found out; can they hypothesise; predict?
	Mixed ability groups (each working with one variable)	6. Demonstrate process of planting seeds; explain the needs to vary the conditions to find out what helps seeds to grow. 7. Ask pupils to suggest how they will check progress and record results.	In groups, plant seeds in a variety of conditions: 1. With both light and water. 2. With light but without water. 3. With water but without light. 4. Pupils may decide to try further tests, e.g. can seeds grow without soil? Decide how to measure and record findings. Measure and record accurately.	Cress seeds. Soil. Water. Measuring equipment (height, time). Recording materials. Cubes or other non-standard measure – ruler – time chart – recording chart or other materials.	Ask groups to report back to the class, using their recorded findings. Assess oral, written and other recorded responses.
	More able pupils in an extension group	Ask pupils to suggest how they will measure growth, check progress and record results.			

Figure 2.2: Planning grid for Life Processes and Living Things

to children, and help teachers to identify what children will be able to learn next.

Diagnosis

It is clear, then, that the teacher's skill in diagnosing her pupils' learning needs is fundamental to successful planning. Neville Bennett (1994) considers diagnosis to be the cornerstone of effective pupil development, quoting Ausobel's view (1968) that the single most important factor influencing learning is what the learner already knows. Bennett considers that much of the assessment in contemporary classrooms takes the form of ticks, crosses or brief comments, but there is little in the way of diagnosis; and that teachers often concentrate on what pupils produce, for example a page of sums, rather than on how these were done. Accurate diagnosis of what pupils already know and understand is essential for the class teacher to provide work which matches their stages of learning, and which allows just the right amount of challenge to reach what Vygotsky (1978) refers to as the 'zone of optimal development'. Caroline Gipps (1992) explains this as:

> the gap that exists for children between what they can do alone and what they can do with help from someone more knowledgeable or skilled than themselves.

This suggests, therefore that the role of the teacher or other adult in the classroom, is crucial for children's learning, and needs to be specifically planned. In particular, the use of language is an important tool in helping children to interact with and consolidate new learning. (Gipps, 1992, Britton, 1989, Edwards and Mercer, 1989)

The importance of language

This is why I have included in the suggested planning model (Figure 2.2) the specific planning of *questions* for a range of purposes: to ascertain what the children already know about the topic; to tease out further explanation from the pupils which encourages them to reflect on what they know from different perspectives; to lead them to consider new ideas or form their own questions; to develop their thinking; to extend their learning; and to consolidate their understanding.

As the teacher gets to know her pupils she will also be able to ask questions of different levels of complexity of individual pupils, based on their ability and learning needs. In the busy classroom, often with large numbers of pupils, the class teacher cannot possibly always plan for every individual child's characteristics (Gipps, op. cit.), but if she plans specific questions or lines of discussion for particular ability groups or to motivate a reluctant learner in one or two areas of work each day she will be going a long way to helping those pupils achieve at suitably challenging levels over time. I saw a good

21

example of this in a Year 6 class recently, where the class were recording the characteristics of inner-city wild-life such as pigeons and foxes, following a class lesson. One recalcitrant pupil, clearly finding nothing in the lesson which appealed to him, was settling down to distracting his neighbours with a series of annoyances, when the teacher drew his attention to a picture of a greyhound in a class library book. Knowing that the boy's uncle owned some greyhounds and that he often helped with their grooming, the teacher used this to overcome the boy's indifference to the topic by encouraging him, first to talk, and then to write about the dogs in a way which displayed his evident interest.

It is also important to plan to introduce *specific vocabulary* and to use it regularly in the context of new learning. In mathematics, for example, pupils need to become very familiar with correct mathematical terms and to be able to use mathematical language with understanding in order to make their way successfully through the programme of study. In the same vein I recently saw a good history lesson where Year 4 pupils looked closely at a set of pictures showing different modes of transport over time. The pupils' interpretations of history from the pictures were of a high standard, prompted by good, open questioning by the teacher, which encouraged children to speculate about what was happening; who were the people, where were they going; what were the features of the picture which identified the era, what was the artist trying to show us? The teacher's persistent use of the correct terminology to describe the modes of transport in the pictures, and his expectation that the pupils also would use accurate vocabulary, helped to consolidate the language and the understanding of work the pupils had been doing earlier in geography, on the same topic. Significantly, this teacher's planning listed the vocabulary to be taught and the questions to be explored during the study of the photographs. He was also teaching them about historical enquiry, close observation and the use of secondary sources of evidence.

Planning pupil groups

In his study of Leeds classrooms Robin Alexander (1992) found much to be concerned about in the ways in which teachers organised group work. Of particular concern was the complexity of organisation, where different groups worked in different curriculum areas simultaneously. HMI (DES, 1990) also expressed concern about classes where too many groups of activities were running at the same time, or where teachers attempted to emphasise individual work which could not be sustained in sufficient depth for all children in the class. These concerns led to the cry for more class teaching, a theme which was repeated in the 'Worlds Apart?' (OFSTED; Reynolds and Farrell, 1996) Review of International Surveys of Educational Achievement, where the superior performance of pupils in Pacific Rim countries was attributed to, among other things, high quantities of whole-class interactive instruction. There is no doubt that well-constructed class lessons which take account of the levels of understanding of all pupils in the class are effective. But the class teacher needs a repertoire of groupings and styles to meet the great range of pupil and curricular needs of the classroom.

The most important factor in her decisions about grouping pupils is *why?* What is to be taught and to whom? What form of grouping will be most effective? Should the pupils be grouped by ability, by social group, by age, or by behaviour? Should the teacher consider the gender or ethnicity of pupils when organising them into groups? How should the pupils' work be organised within groups to be successful?

The teacher needs to consider all of these factors when making decisions about grouping pupils for learning. A teacher who organises groups flexibly, to match the particular aspect of the curriculum or the pupils, is clearly demonstrating that she is starting from what and how pupils need to learn when planning their work.

Grouping children by ability or even for social harmony within one subject area is one strategy used by teachers. It has the advantage of focusing all pupils on the same topic, albeit at different stages, which makes it easier for the teacher to teach specific points to the whole class, and for pupils to compare what they have been learning with other groups when they come together as a class to talk about what they have learned.

Pupils working in two or more subject areas in groups is another common strategy, but research evidence (Alexander, op. cit.; Mortimore *et al.*, 1988) suggests that good teaching and learning are more difficult to sustain in this situation, as it requires a high level of teacher organisation and skill, pupils who can work independently for extended periods, and a well-structured learning environment, to be fully effective. Many teachers find all of these features difficult to achieve consistently, and research (Alexander, op. cit.) has shown that teachers have fewer interactions with children, that pupils themselves spend large amounts of time talking amongst themselves about things not related to work, and that pupils in classes which are organised in this way for most of the time tend to make slow progress.

Some teachers set work for individual pupils, and move round groups giving individual support. Studies of pupil/teacher contact in these situations have shown it to be least effective in terms of pupils' progress (Mortimore, op. cit.; HMI, 1985) because interactions tend to be too infrequent and superficial for effective learning. It also provides too few opportunities for pupils to learn from each other. For the same reasons teachers must also be wary of providing too many individual worksheets or of expecting pupils to work through published schemes unquestioningly. Many of these concerns can be overcome by making sure that there are lots of opportunities for pupils to discuss their work with each other and with the teacher, and that the teacher's interactions with specific pupils or groups are planned, and have a clear learning focus.

When children are taught how to work collaboratively in groups their learning can be very effective. Genuinely collaborative group work can encourage children's social development, their skills in decision-making, negotiating, co-operating and in taking responsibility. It can also help children learn successfully from each other. Joan Dean (1992) considers that 'training' in group work skills is a normal part of life in an infant classroom, where children learn to share, take turns, listen to other people and try to see their point of view. The teacher of older pupils needs to continue this 'training', working consciously at developing these skills, occasionally praising children for their successful work in the group, showing that it is valued.

The reflective teacher

I have argued in this chapter that planning for learning demands that the teacher knows the pupils. This means knowing their characteristics and personalities as well as their learning styles and levels of ability. To get the best out of children the teacher needs to know them as people. The teacher needs to become increasingly more skilled in observing, assessing and reflecting on the learning of her pupils if she is to develop her understanding of how best to help them, and develop her expertise as a teacher. Top-down models of staff development often do not take into account the teacher as a person (Fullan and Hargreaves, 1991). Some of the most effective teacher development occurs when teachers themselves are in control, for example through some form of action-research, however informally organised.

One teacher that I know uses a structured observation process in her own classroom, deciding for herself the focus of her research. She keeps a running diary entirely for her own use, and uses her reflections on this to discuss her developing thinking with a colleague. She sometimes has another adult in the classroom, which helps her to plan an observation. The observation and reflection focus can be limited to, say, individual pupils or a particular classroom activity; it might include the children's behaviour and attitudes within certain situations, such as when sharing equipment, or in particular areas of the curriculum such as PE. It will include consideration of their relationships with each other; how they work together in groups; whether there are issues surrounding gender or ethnicity in the way particular groups go about their learning and in how well they achieve. The teacher has changed what she does in the classroom as a result of this reflection, and has been amazed by the positive impact her changed approach has had on pupils' learning. Her deeper knowledge of the children as people enables her to plan more successfully the work she provides and the ways in which she groups and teaches the pupils. Other teachers in the school have become interested and now the school as a whole is developing an 'action-research' approach to professional development, designed to encourage reflective teachers.

Conclusion

Successful planning is at the heart of good teaching. In today's schools the process is essentially collaborative, involving all staff at some stage. The class teacher has the responsibility for matching the planned curriculum to the pupils in her class, according to their existing experience, their aptitudes, knowledge and skills, and what they need to learn next. Planning for learning, rather than simply to cover the curriculum, is a complex process demanding skill, knowledge of the curriculum, a sound understanding of the children, and a healthy questioning and reflective attitude to teaching and learning on the part of the teacher.

In the course of her planning the teacher must take account of the different learning needs of the pupils, including those with special educational needs. The teacher's weekly and daily planning should include specific provision for pupils who have a statement of special educational need or an individual education plan (IEP) under the Code of Practice (Education Act, 1993). The work provided and the level of support for these pupils should reflect that which is described in their IEPs or statement.

Teaching styles, classroom organisation and pupil groupings need to be given careful consideration when planning for learning; and in the context of the subject curriculum the class teacher can do no better than to plan specifically for children to have many opportunities to talk about their work, to ask questions as well as answer them, reflect upon and explain what they are doing and why.

Finally, the teacher who undertakes a critical analysis of her own work and of her pupils' responses through observation and reflection empowers herself as a thinking, creative professional. This places her in a strong position to understand children well enough to 'do honour to their rights and interests' in the educational process (Drummond, 1994).

References

Alexander, R. (1992), *Policy and Practice in Primary Education*, Routledge.

Ausobel, D.P. (1968), *Educational Psychology: A Cognitive View*, Holt, Rinehart & Winston.

Bennett, N. (1992), *Managing Learning in the Primary Classroom (ASPE Paper 1)*, ASPE/Trentham Books.

Britton, J. (1989), 'Vygotsky's Contribution to Pedagogical Theory', in Murphy, P. and Moon, B. (eds), *Developments in Learning and Assessment*, Hodder & Stoughton.

Clay, M.M. (1993), *Reading Recovery: An Observation Survey of Early Literacy Achievement*, Heinemann.

Dean, J. (1983, 1992), *Organising Learning in the Primary Classroom*, Routledge.

DES (1990), *The Teaching and Learning of Reading in Primary Schools: A Report by HMI*, HMSO.

DfEE (1995), *The National Curriculum 1988*, HMSO.

Drummond, M.J. (1993), *Assessing Children's Learning,* David Fulton Publishers.

Edwards, D. and Mercer, N. (1989), *Common Knowledge,* Routledge.

Fullan, M. and Hargreaves, A. (1991), *What's Worth Fighting for in Your School?,* Open University Press.

Gipps, C. (1992), *What We Know About Effective Primary Teaching,* University of London Institute of Education.

Mortimore, P., Sammons, P., Stoll, L., Lewis, D. and Ecob, R. (1988), *School Matters: The Junior School Years,* Open Books.

Office for Standards in Education (1995a), *Framework for Inspections,* HMSO.

Office for Standards in Education (1995b), *Guidance on the Inspection of Nursery and Primary Schools,* HMSO.

Office for Standards in Education (1996), *Subjects & Standards: Issues for School Development Arising from OFSTED Inspection Findings 1994-5: Key Stages 1 & 2,* HMSO.

Proctor, A., Entwhistle, M., Judge, B. and McKenzie-Murdoch, S. (1995), *Learning to Teach in the Primary Classroom,* Routledge.

Reynolds, D. and Farrell, S. (1996), *Worlds Apart?: A Review of International Surveys of Educational Achievement Involving England,* OFSTED/HMSO.

Schools Curriculum and Assessment Authority (1995), *Planning the Curriculum at Key Stages 1 and 2,* SCAA.

3

■ ■ ■

Assessment, Recording and Reporting

ROSE COLLINSON

It is helpful, at least in relation to assessment, recording and reporting, to think about what is legal, desirable and manageable.

- Legal – the have to do's.
- Desirable – the want to do's.
- Manageable – making it work on a day-to-day basis in the classroom.

Assessment, like Topsy, has just growed over the last few years. In some schools it has begun to seem more like the ongoing demolition of a tropical rainforest than an essential aspect of children's learning, progress and achievement. Busy classroom teachers can end up feeling as though they have got a tame Murray Walker, the Formula One racing commentator, imprisoned in their head saying faster and faster in his own inimitable style, 'There's still more to do; you haven't done enough.' The principle and practice of manageable assessment seems as complicated as the White Queen in *Alice through the Looking Glass* believing as many as six impossible things before breakfast.

This chapter aims to explain the big picture of assessment by breaking it down into manageable chunks or aspects and offer ways in which it can work in your classroom. A shift from Alice's impossibilities to John Ruskin's 1851 thoughts:

> *In order that people may be happy in their work, these three things are needed: they must be fit for it; they must not do too much of it; and they must have a sense of success in it.*

Translating that into up-to-date assessment practice it means assessing less, but doing it well and targeting the assessment you do to find out about the learning you've planned.

The big picture

Assessment has tended to generate its own jargon and vocabulary. Self-assessment, for example, always seems to make more sense than ipsative assessment. However, one person's plain speaking is another's bureaucratic jargon and it's useful to remember Dearing's common-sense definitions (SCAA, 1994).

Assessment is the judgement teachers make about a child's attainment based on knowledge gained through techniques such as observation, questioning, marking pieces of work and testing.

Recording is teachers making a record of significant attainments to inform curriculum planning and reports to parents or others. It is not possible or sensible to attempt to record all the information collected. Much of it will, necessarily, remain in the teacher's mind.

Reporting is the process of informing others, including the parents, headteachers, governors, the child's next teacher or school and the child. Records of children's attainments should be useful when preparing their reports.

Linking those definitions, which emphasise:

- using a range of assessment techniques and approaches that fit the purpose;
- trusting professional judgement to decide what needs to be recorded and which bits of information need to be passed on; and
- integrating planning, assessment, recording and reporting so each process helps the next;

to a set of principles which make sense in your school and classroom can help sort out what, in practice, you really mean by using assessment to support and improve learning. Many schools have found looking at assessment from the perspectives of children, teachers and parents a useful starting point.

In *our school* children have an entitlement to an assessment process which:

- accurately identifies and tracks their progress;
- highlights strengths and difficulties together with strategies to manage them;
- raises the expectation of success and celebrates a broad range of achievements;
- provides reliable and credible information to support learning; and
- is motivating and actively involves them in review and target setting.

In *our school* teachers have an entitlement to assessment and recording procedures which:

- are based on clear and shared criteria;
- are manageable, sustainable, consistent and useful;

- meet statutory requirements;
- support quality teaching and learning; and
- produce reliable and valid assessments.

From *our school* parents have an entitlement to assessment and reporting practices which:

- highlight their child's success and progress;
- identify weaknesses and explains how they will be addressed;
- provide them with opportunities to review and discuss their child's achievements;
- involve them in helping to meet learning targets; and
- ensure information about their child is detailed, specific and easy to understand.

Your own school policy statement may operate on different principles but as Ruth Sutton (1995) so succinctly puts it:

> ... *it's worth asking regularly the fundamental assessment question: why are we doing this assessment, and who is it for? Does what we actually do, or propose to do, match with this purpose and audience?*

It is easy to talk glibly about assessment being a holistic, formative process which is an integral part of teaching and learning. Although I really believe it makes enormous sense to link planning, assessing, recording, and reporting, it is helpful initially to sort it out into chunks, work out what is going well and what else needs developing and how it links together to make sense in your classroom and school.

The have to do's

What are the legal requirements? What about end of key stage assessments? How do the OFSTED criteria fit in?

Despite what you might imagine, the statutory requirements concerning assessment are actually fairly minimal. However, it is important that every teacher, whether or not she is teaching a Year 2 or Year 6 class, knows about them, understands their implications and keeps up to date with any changes. What you have to do is:

- Keep an individual record:
  - for each child;
  - update it at least once a year;
  - there is, however, no prescribed format;

- levels are only required in English, maths and science at the end of the key stage.
- Report to parents annually with a written report containing:
  - brief particulars of all National Curriculum subjects and RE;
  - attendance information;
  - consultation arrangements; and
  - at the end of a key stage (and only then) provide core subject levels for both teacher assessment and tasks/tests, school comparative results and national comparative figures for the previous year.
- Complete the statutory requirement to transfer end of key stage information.
- Report end of key stage results in the school prospectus and Governors' annual report to parents.

There are no quotas set for each of the National Curriculum levels and no underlying assumptions about the proportion of pupils who should be at any particular level. A typical seven-year-old is expected to achieve level 2; a typical 11-year-old level 4.

At Key Stage 1 most pupils will be operating within the range of levels 1–3 and at Key Stage 2 within levels 2–5. End of key stage descriptions in art, music and PE equate broadly to level 2 at Key Stage 1 and level 4 at Key Stage 2.

In terms of National Curriculum requirements the Programmes of Study (PoS) are the basis for planning, teaching and ongoing assessment. Over the key stage, all the PoS have to be taught but there is no requirement to assess every single aspect of them. Equally, apart from the requirement to keep records updated annually on every child's academic achievements, other skills and abilities and progress, there are no requirements about how or in what form records should be kept. Decisions about how to mark work and record progress are professional matters for the school as a whole to consider in the context of the needs of their children.

Therefore it is down to us as educational professionals to discuss and come to an agreed view about what and how learning should be assessed in each subject/area of experience so that over time, over a key stage, it is possible to draw on a whole (but not excessive) range of ongoing assessment information, records and evidence to come to a professional 'best fit' judgement about attainment against 'level descriptions' or 'end of key stage descriptions'.

How do you keep up to date about the 'have to do's'. Schools receive circulars from DfEE explaining and updating any requirements. The assessment arrangements for the end of each key stage are published usually each autumn.

Testing times

If you teach Year 2 and Year 6 children then it is particularly important to understand the detail of the end of key stage assessment arrangements. Each year published guidance explains which children should be assessed; the teacher assessment requirements; the structure and timing of the National Curriculum tasks and tests; key dates; special arrangements; and, in the case of Key Stage 1, the audit requirements and, for Key Stage 2, the external marking arrangements. Whatever the specific detail it is important to remember that there are two elements to end of key stage arrangements: Teacher Assessment and National Tests/Tasks. They both have equal status and do different though complementary jobs.

Teacher assessment identifies achievements over time while tests provide a snapshot of attainment at a particular point in time. Tests sample some aspects of a subject; teacher assessment judgements are based on achievements across the whole programme of study. For example, at the end of Key Stage 2, what is tested is children's ability to write to time and task but ability to draft is assessed by teacher assessment. Tests by their very nature tend to be structured, written assessments giving children a limited range of opportunities to show what they know, understand and can do, whereas teacher assessments, built up over time, are based on a variety of evidence (what children say, do, make, ask, write about) in a range of contexts on a number of occasions. Teacher assessment makes the black and white, potentially fuzzy, test snapshot into a much more panoramic and credible video.

Baseline assessment for children entering reception classes will become a statutory requirement in September 1998. Many schools already engage in some form of baseline assessment to:

- get to know children's strengths and learning needs;
- inform future planning; and
- involve parents and carers.

The national framework will cover aspects of language and literacy, mathematics and personal and social development and link to desirable outcomes.

The OFSTED view

The OFSTED Handbook (1995), while supporting the principle of assessment as an integral part of teaching and learning is thin on what it might actually look like in practice. However, the key questions are useful to think about in relation to your school and your classroom.

Do teachers assess pupils' work thoroughly and constructively, and use assessments to inform teaching?

In other words, have you shared the learning objectives and assessment criteria with pupils and do they know what they need to do to improve their work and make progress.

Are there effective systems for assessing pupils' attainment? Is assessment information used to inform curriculum planning?

In other words, are assessments and records useful *and* used? Are you responding to what your assessments are telling you?

A check should be made on how parents are kept informed about their child's progress, including whether written reports to parents meet the statutory requirements and give clear information about pupils' attainment and progress.

In other words, are they specific and easy to interpret, explaining achievement, progress and next steps clearly and without jargon?

So what do you need to remember about the have to do's?

- Be up to date with the actual requirements not the myths about what someone else thinks might be necessary.
- Remember the complementary but different purposes of teacher assessment and tasks/tests.
- Make use of and apply any special arrangements individual children need.
- Judgements against level descriptions are about typical performance (on a good day, when the hamster hasn't died and life's all right at home, Jo Bloggs is usually able to/understands/knows about . . .).
- Be prepared to learn from end of key stage assessments – if all the children struggled with the writing tasks then it is worth asking whether progression in writing is clearly enough addressed in long and medium term planning? Is there enough emphasis throughout the key stage on talking and writing about writing and writers? Is enough time given for experimenting with different forms and functions of writing? Does writing regularly leave the classroom (e.g. letters being sent)? Is there enough practice in writing within time limits?

The want to do's

Once the 'have to do's' are sorted out, then it is easier to focus on what we want and would like to do. It is probably helpful to start thinking about assessment in relation to:

- Looking for learning
  - planning assessment into learning;

- – having clear, shared criteria;
- – building on previous learning and making connections with what comes next.
- Remembering learning
  - – making decisions about what to record and what to pass on;
  - – gathering evidence;
  - – developing children's abilities and skills in setting and meeting learning targets;
  - – giving feedback and marking.
- Celebrating learning
  - – reporting;
  - – ensuring consistency.
- Monitoring and evaluating
  - – asking is it working and how do we know?

Curriculum planning is now fairly well established in schools. Most teachers recognise the three levels of planning outlined in SCAA's *Planning the Curriculum at Key Stage 1 and 2.*

Long-term planning provides the big picture, it is the broad overview of a whole school map of the child's learning and experiences in school. It identifies how the National Curriculum and other school priorities will be covered and enables teachers to plot curriculum continuity and progression and consider breadth, balance and coherence.

Medium-term, termly or half-termly planning develops the use of long-term key stage plans into more specific programmes of work for a particular year group. These deal at a much more practical level with the knowledge, skills and understanding to be developed in each subject or curriculum area. This is where there is a feel for the 'pitch' or level of demand and where the assessment opportunities are identified.

Short-term planning is more easily understood as planning what happens on day-to-day or weekly basis in your classrooms – most people understand it as teaching! – i.e. knowing which children are doing which task and how you intend to assess.

Assessment features significantly at the medium-term level since this is the level to make clear decisions about learning objectives and identify the assessment opportunities which will help you know in practice that they have been achieved by some or all of the children.

Various medium-term formats and headings exist; increasingly they are seen, rightly, as school planning, not something individuals plan and replan each year on their own. In assessment terms it is worth thinking about getting everyone to write down briefly at the end of each term or half-term, jottings on

Planning Level	Involving	To ensure	Outcomes
Long term: key stage plans: the whole school map	**Headteacher and all staff**	• coverage of and progression in all aspects of the whole school curriculum (including the NC across the whole key stage) • balance within and across the subjects/aspects of the curriculum in each year of the key stage • coherence within and between subjects • suitable allocation of time • continuity between key stages	• A broad framework for each year of the key stage reflecting the school's overall curricular aims and objectives • specified subject content • content organised into manageable and coherent units of work • a notional time allocation to each unit of work • logical sensible sequence of work and development of key skills • identified links between aspects of different subjects
Medium term: termly or half-term plans	**Class teachers** supported by co-ordinators/subject leaders	Detailed units of work identifying intended progression and assessment opportunities for each year group	A detailed specification for each unit of work to be taught setting out: • specific learning objectives • emphasis, priorities and depth of treatment • broad resource requirements • pupil tasks and activities • strategies for differentiating work • assessment opportunities
Short term: each week or day	**Class teachers and pupils**	• appropriate classroom organisation, management and teaching strategies • achievement, progress and success for all • a balance of different types of activity throughout a week • differentiation • appropriate pace • time for teacher assessment, pupils' involvement, feedback and review • monitoring, evaluation and (if required) modifications to the medium term plan	• detailed daily or weekly lesson plans • manageable assessment • appropriate records • effective day to day teaching and learning • informed future planning

Figure 3.1: The three levels of curriculum planning
(*Source*: Modified from SCAA, 1995, *Planning the Curriculum at Key Stages 1 & 2*)

what went well and why; what was planned but not taught; so that if, like most primary teachers you wear another hat as curriculum co-ordinator, you can track whether the planned continuity and progression really did work and make any improvements necessary.

Short-term planning for assessment is much easier within a fairly detailed medium planning framework. Having sorted out, in broad terms, what you want children to learn and the kinds of evidence of success in that learning, you will be much clearer about knowing the focus and expectation of the tasks (increasing knowledge?; practising skills?; access to experiences?; developing understanding?) as well as (from previous assessments) what your pupils can already do and what and how you will recognise success.

Crucially, it is about being very clear yourself and making sure the children are clear too about what they are doing; why they are doing it; how long they have got to complete the task and how they can judge their success and progress in it. It may well be you will decide to apply different criteria to different groups of children (Figure 3.2). So for one group the key target will be: 'I have not forgotten any full stops' and 'I have used joining words'. For others the expectation will be to include all the elements in their story. Being clear about what you are looking for highlights the type of assessment methods which are appropriate. Do you need, for example, 'to eavesdrop' on a group; observe, then ask questions; read their work afterwards. It may well be a mix of all these techniques but obviously for some you need to be present at the time, for others it can be done later.

Some teachers when organising their short-term planning find it useful to jot down a brief list of questions they intend asking children to check their knowledge and understanding.

Teachers involved in the London Institute of Education research on Key Stage 1 assessment found observation one of the most helpful assessment methods:

> *You do concentrate, you don't leave people out. You don't assume things.*

Adding, from time to time, brief notes in their teacher planner or day book meant:

> *It's very easy to miss children and this way is much more foolproof – showing you've talked to a child.*

If the learning objective is 'to participate positively in discussion taking some account of others' view' then the assessment criteria might be self or peer group evaluation by everyone in the class, but with you this time, specifically observing one or two groups and making brief notes on their skills in discussion and contribution to group dynamics. If the learning objective is to 'discuss and evaluate reading and refer to relevant passages in support of opinions' then the assessment criteria might be, when marking the written work, the extent to which appropriate references are made to the text. Equally,

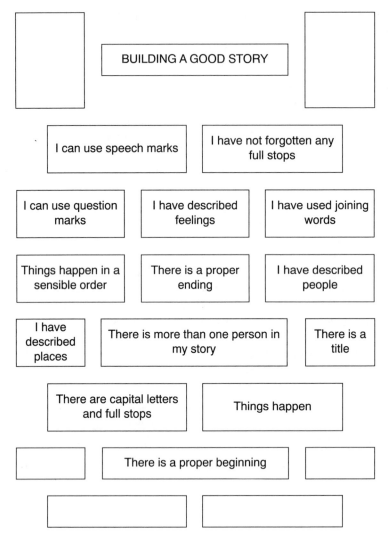

Figure 3.2: Creative writing assessment sheet
(*Source*: Adapted from Nottinghamshire LEA, 1994)

if the learning objective is 'recognition of 2D and 3D shapes' then the assessment criteria might be to match shape names to correct shapes with a classroom assistant or a parent helper.

Remembering learning

The reality of record keeping can often feel like the fantasy of *Bluff your way in Teaching* (Yapp, 1987; 1994):

In record keeping, teachers write down

(a) What was supposed to happen;

(b) What they wish had happened;

(c) What they know will never happen

... desperately trying to find sufficient information to fill six sides of A4 paper about a child of whom you only have the dimmest recollection ...

It's reassuring to remember what Dearing (SCAA, 1994) has to say about record keeping:

Records supplement the teacher's personal knowledge of a child. It is not possible for teachers to record all their knowledge and they should not be tempted to try. Written records complement this professional understanding. If record systems do not provide a significant contribution to teaching and learning there is little point in maintaining them.

Records should be useful, manageable to keep and easy to interpret ... there is no need to keep records that are no longer relevant because they have been superseded by the progress of the child. Neither is there a need to write long narrative descriptions of previously known information, nor to record the same attainment more than once.

Recording and record keeping become much more meaningful and useful if you (and the children) are clear about what you are looking for in their learning. Being clear about what you're expecting gives you more scope to take account of unexpected and unanticipated learning. Children are not, thankfully, pre-programmed with a barcode imprinted in their foreheads which bleeps every time they achieve a learning objective, and frequently they achieve in different ways to those we've planned.

Records have been described as 'taking assessment from mind to paper', but it is important to keep a sense of perspective; paper mountains are not usually re-read by their creator and are frequently ignored by the next person.

Curriculum plans outline teaching intentions, learning outcomes and assessment opportunities so there is no need to repeat all of that. In practice, records, marking and feedback:

- help to keep track of achievements, progress, judgements and next steps;
- help children to know how they are getting on; and what else they need to do; and
- from time to time, can be drawn on to provide a summary for the parents, for the next teacher or the next school.

Many Northumberland nursery and first schools use an Early Years Record of Achievement as a mechanism to build on (Northumberland LEA, 1994), to acknowledge and value the home-school partnership, and to provide a manageable way of planning learning and setting targets. Skills and achievement 'stickers' record progress as well as celebrate individual achievement. Examples include:

'I can draw somebody with a body.'

'I can hold scissors properly.'

'I know today/yesterday/tomorrow.'

'I can make patterns longer.'

'I can talk about what I am tasting.'

To ones that many parents will readily recognise:

'I can have my hair washed without crying.'

'I can sleep in my own bed all night.'

Other early years teachers and support staff have found it helpful to note down observations of learning or regression on 'Post-Its', discuss them at a convenient point, then stick them in an individual book or file under areas of the curriculum and tick them off on an overall class or group chart. Many Kent schools find the following questions useful as starting points for checking that their records really are useful and used:

- How much detail do you need to record?
- Do you want to record all subjects/aspects of the whole curriculum in the same way?
- Would it be more appropriate and useful in some areas of learning to record the attainment of individuals, groups, classes?

In a group record sheet, for example, you might have three columns: one to list the names of those children who achieved all the planned learning objectives and worked with extension activities; another for those who met the criteria but didn't move onto extension work and another to highlight those children who need further support and help to understand and grasp the key ideas and skills.

Other teachers find it more helpful to have one record per child, with all the subjects listed and room to record significant progress and development and next steps. This kind of record is frequently supplemented by some more detailed comments and observations on AT1.

- Do you plan to keep individual pupil portfolios?
- To what extent and how will children be involved in self-assessment, peer assessment, target setting and review?
- What information would you want to receive as the next teacher?
- Do children with Special Educational Needs require different and/or additional records?
- Do you plan to summarise children's achievement within the key stage?

Some schools find it helpful to break down the level descriptions into their key points and at the end of a unit of work in, for example, English or history, to highlight attainment (not coverage) by an individual child. This kind of record can be very useful to set targets with children and help explain to parents what their child has achieved *and* what else they need to do, and show in a very concrete way just how broad the expectations of a level are.

- How will your records contribute to the reporting requirements?

Giving feedback and marking

Marking and giving feedback has to be much more than 'satisfactory; but you can do better'. Whatever our age we all need to know how well we're getting on and what else we need to do to improve. Frequently its not just about 'telling' either orally or in writing but about being shown and seeing our attempts set out correctly, looking at other pupils' work; or working alongside other children or adults. We tend to 'believe' feedback if it is constructive and honest. Marking and feedback which is of the bland 'well done, this is a lovely story' or 'good work' type doesn't tell me whether the story is perfect or how good the work is. Exhortations such as 'presentation!'; 'paragraphs!'; or 'spelling!', don't explain whether all or only some of it is at fault and the well-worn 'you must try harder' doesn't explain what I've got to do since it is likely that if I knew I'd have tried to get it right in the first place. At best those kinds of comments are unclear; at worst unhelpful.

> *Learning is well supported when pupils are aware of what they are trying to achieve in particular pieces of work and when, through careful marking, they have a clear picture about what they have done well and what they need to do better next time.*
>
> *(OFSTED, 1995)*

Marking and feedback is an essential part of assessment because it is about focusing attention on practical ways to improve children's learning and helping them to understand their progress and achievements. It is important to think about purposes and although checking that work has been done is a legitimate purpose, there must be an emphasis on constructive feedback about what has been done, how well it has been done and what else needs to be done to improve.

It's most useful if you think about the marking focus at the planning stage; if the focus is on correcting errors and ensuring accuracy then ticks and crosses may be sufficient, but if the focus is drafting and developing content, structure and expression or responding to other readers' opinions, then comments need to be evaluative, for example:

> *'I like this image/this paragraph but are there other words you can use to make this livelier/more interesting.'*

> *'Have you thought about other words you can use instead of "said" or "got"?'*

Although giving the children opportunities to apply criteria and mark each other's work is valuable it is also important that as a teacher, you have an overview of attainment and progress which means, in addition, regularly looking at everyone's work and giving guidance on how to improve.

Agreeing how frequent feedback should be is an essential part of marking; it's very demotivating if your work isn't looked at and written on or talked about. However, attempting to mark everything is a recipe for overload; being specific at the planning stage and sharing and explaining the criteria for success with children should mean that the workload is manageable and you and they know how they are getting on and what the next steps are.

The 'next steps' can be noted on your records or in the back of the children's folders or work book. The latter can help develop children's abilities and skills in thinking and talking about their learning. In 'mark' terms it is understanding why you got the '7' as well as what else would help towards the '10'. During a unit of work the next steps will be short, specific and typically linked to ongoing work. If the focus is using correct maths vocabulary to describe shapes, e.g. 'edges' or 'corners', a target for some children might be to use more specific language and mathematical criteria. Next steps in ongoing work (in SCAA's terminology, the continuous units – the drip feed bits of the curriculum which happen regularly and frequently) are much easier to specify and do something about since there are lots of opportunities to practise and consolidate skills and understanding. Specifying targets in blocked units – the stand-alone, content-heavy topics – can be more difficult since revising or revisiting that particular bit of knowledge may be with another teacher in another school. Setting broad learning skills targets is more useful in this instance.

Self and peer assessment

One of the skills children are increasingly going to need in their learning and their lives is that of being able to recognise their own achievements and evaluate their own learning. Like all skills it needs practise, support and a vocabulary which extends beyond the 'I must try harder' syndrome.

If self and peer assessment is going to work, children actually need to understand what is expected of them (although I fondly remember the six-year-old dashing off to the next activity which happened to be Design and Technology and when asked what he was going to do next, solemnly looked up and said 'I don't know, Miss, but it's lovely here 'cos it's all a surprise!'). Some teachers find it useful to break down the PoS into small steps.

'I measured rather than guessed what was happening.'

'Things happen in a sensible order in my story.'

'I can explain my route home to someone else.'

When the targets and expectations are clear then it is about planning opportunities to practise and use them: for example, joint editing of a story; a collaborative project or some independent work can provide scope for children to write or talk about what they consider their successes (I've achieved); their efforts (I've tried hard at); their improvement (I'm better at). It also from time to time (say twice a year) might feed into a one-to-one review about achievement, progress and next steps.

When targets are set they do need to be SMART:

Specific	– What exactly do I need to do;
Measurable	– I'll know when I've done it;
Achievable	– I believe I can do it;
Realistic	– It makes sense to me;
Timed	– I'm going to be successful in this by . . .

Reporting to parents

Thankfully, we have moved on a long way from the 'satisfactory; must try harder' one liners that we may have received at school as well as the somewhat cynical and hopefully apocryphal:

1940s leaving report: *'Lavinia will do well so long as she avoids gin and Polish officers.'*

Exam paper: *'5%. This mark reveals gaps in his ignorance.'*

Comment on a reference: Leadership skills: *'The only reason to follow this boy into battle would be through a morbid sense of curiosity.'*

School report: *'The improvement in Tracy's handwriting has served to reveal her appalling spelling.'*

Good reports are economical, informative and:

- explain what the child has learned, not just what he/she has been taught;
- are written for parents and children, without jargon, and in a way which will motivate children over the next year;
- have a balance between comments about pupils' activities and personal skills and information about their attainment and progress;
- provide a summary of performance since the last report highlighting achievement and progress; identifying weaknesses and areas for development and recommending some achievable short-term targets.

Parents welcome informal and written reports especially when they explain ways in which they can help their children (such as reading with them or practising maths concepts, e.g. how many pairs of socks have you got at home?).

Gloucester's guidance to schools (1996) has some good examples:

> *I am pleased with the progress that Susan has made this year and her work now matches the targets for her age-group. She reads well and fluently and tackles difficult books with enthusiasm. Her ability to write well-constructed stories, however, has not developed quite as well because she does not ask for help as often as she might.*

> *John's work in maths has disappointed me this year. Although he approaches maths projects with enthusiasm, he doesn't bring enough care to the way he presents his work and consequently makes mistakes. He has a quick brain and can calculate accurately and confidently when dealing with really quite complicated problems involving large numbers. Overall, however, his general carelessness has held back his progress in other aspects of maths, particularly those involving work on shape and space.*

What is important in all reporting is the use you make of your ongoing records. They should provide you with the information to summarise. As well as keeping specific subject records some teachers find it helpful to have a section in their mark book (or a set of small file cards or an exercise book with a space for each child) to note down things about particular children as and when they occur using codes or words (whichever suit you best). At regular intervals, you do need to check which children you have missed out. In any class the able and the children who find learning difficult tend to have much more written about them than the 'invisible', frequently fairly quiet and compliant children. Your jottings help to build up an individual picture of each child which should contribute significantly towards their report.

Consistency

Clearly it is in everyone's interest, especially children's, to make sure that we apply the standards agreed within the school consistently in our classrooms and that our standards are comparable to other schools. In the early days of National Curriculum 'agreement trialling' was a fairly new concept which easily moved, in practice, into disagreement trials where the body language tended to be arms folded and people thinking, but certainly not saying, 'Well, that wouldn't be level three in my classroom.' *Saying* is really the operative word for establishing consistency since it is only by starting to talk about work that we can begin to really share standards. Consistency doesn't come about because of a national set of programmes of study but through discussion. Some of the collections of annotated work produced by SCAA can help kick start the discussion and help towards a collaborative decision about the level of demand of an aspect of a PoS. Other things that help consistency include many activities we now take for granted in primary schools such as:

- joint planning between teachers;
- developing common activities focused on agreed objectives;
- discussing and marking children's work together to develop shared expectations of performance;
- comparing the performance of children from different classes on common activities;
- looking at samples of children's work from a range of contexts relating to a particular level description or end of key stage description.

One outcome of these kinds of activities might be a collection of material; a school portfolio which is a way of collecting together samples and sets of work with a brief explanation/annotation showing how they reflect national standards.

Monitoring and evaluation

Monitoring is the 'in' word at INSET. It has almost taken over from 'differentiation' but what does it mean in practice. A definition that works for me and is practical is:

- *Monitoring* asks the question: *Is it working?*
- *Evaluation* is the judgement you are able to make from time to time: *Is it working well?*
- *Monitoring* is about checking: *Are we doing what we said we would do?*
- *Evaluation* focuses on asking: *Is what we are doing effective?*

It is useful to think of the assessment policy being the document which *says what we do*. Assessment practice means all of us *doing what we say*.

Consistency in assessment is about being able to *show and share what we do*, and monitoring and evaluation is *making sure it is working . . . well*.

Practical ways of monitoring include using the annual publication from OFSTED/DfEE, *Subjects and Standards – issues for school development arising from OFSTED inspection findings*. This has a double-page spread for each subject giving the main findings nationally and key issues for schools (assessment is a frequent key issue!). Examples include in English, for example:

> *Finding ways of keeping effective and useful records, particularly of progress in reading is a priority for many schools.*

The Association for Assessment Inspectors and Advisers publishes a very useful broadsheet (AAIA, 1996) which breaks down assessment into manageable sections:

- long, medium and short-term planning;

- ongoing assessment;
- marking and feedback to pupils;
- end of key stage assessment;
- recording and evidence;
- reporting;
- transferring;
- using assessment information and results; and
- managing and monitoring assessment, recording and reporting.

Each of these has some key points to help schools identify good practice. It's a very reassuring and practical guide to help work out what is going well and what else might need to be developed. A brief flavour of the reporting section is that reporting is working well when reports to parents and carers:

- provide clear information that parents can understand about their children's progress outlining strengths and the areas they need to develop;
- set realistic targets that are worked on and reviewed.

Another helpful tool for evaluation is analysis of end of key stage assessment outcomes and asking questions to check whether:

- expectations in our school are appropriate for all pupils;
- there is improvement in relation to our baseline;
- boys and girls are achieving similar results;
- some classes are performing better than others;
- there are variations in performance in different subjects;
- pupils here do as well as pupils in similar schools elsewhere;
- we know what we do well;
- there are any year-on-year trends.

For example, did we place enough emphasis throughout the key stage on skimming and scanning to find out information? Did we give enough time to the skill of explaining, not merely describing, in all subjects?

Making assessment work for you

First of all by keeping assessment in perspective – assess less but do it well and talk about learning more – might be a useful maxim, i.e. be more focused and precise about what you're looking for in learning and share expectations and standards. Teachers have always assessed and made judgements about children's progress, achievements and next steps. The difference in the last few years has been that we now have a National Curriculum *and* associated assessment criteria, which means when we are planning what we want children to learn we have assessment in mind, and that it is in there by design not default. Remember above all when making decisions about what and how to assess and record that:

- information should be useful and *used*;
- much, but certainly not everything, can be remembered;
- some information, but not all, needs to be passed on.

It can be done!

References

Association of Assessment Inspectors and Advisers (1996), *Teacher Assessment in Action*, AAIA.

Gloucestershire LEA (1996), *Using Assessment to Inform Planning*, Gloucestershire County Council.

Northumberland LEA (1994), *Recording Achievement Together*, Northumberland County Council.

Nottinghamshire LEA (1994), *Developing Children's Skills in Review, Self Assessment and Target Setting*, Nottinghamshire County Council.

OFSTED (1995), *The OFSTED Handbook*, HMSO.

OFSTED/DfEE (1996), *Subjects and Standards: Issues for School Development*, HMSO.

Schools Curriculum and Assessment Authority (1994), *The National Curriculum and its Assessment*, SCAA.

Schools Curriculum and Assessment Authority (1995), *Planning the Curriculum at Key Stages 1 and 2*, SCAA.

Sutton, R. (1995), *Assessment for Learning*, RS Publications.

Yapp, M. (1987:1994), *Bluff Your Way in Teaching*, Lavette Books.

4

■ ■ ■

Grouping Pupils to Meet Individual Needs

PAUL SMITH

Group-work has often been seen as one of the essential features of a modern primary classroom. From the sixties onwards it became increasingly rare to find children sitting at traditional desks arranged in neat straight rows. More commonly they were grouped together around a set of tables, facing one another rather than the blackboard or the teacher. There was an assumption that group-work was a 'good thing', part of the primary ethos which encouraged children to work collaboratively, co-operating rather than competing, and benefiting from the knowledge and skills of their peers. Unfortunately just sitting together does not necessarily guarantee that children are working as a group or learning any more effectively. This point was highlighted in a recent publication, *Subjects and Standards* (OFSTED, 1996):

> ... *genuine collaborative work is rare. Particularly in mathematics, reading and topic work, pupils predominantly work individually and at their own pace. There is evidence to suggest that schools should be more vigilant about the amount of individual work undertaken in subjects such as mathematics. When carried to an extreme, this leaves pupils with too little opportunity to benefit from in-depth explanation and questioning by the teacher or from discussion with other pupils.*

The current debate on raising educational standards has perhaps inevitably seen a resurgence of interest in more 'traditional' approaches to classroom management, particularly a greater use of whole-class teaching and the setting or streaming of pupils by ability. Of course most teachers have always used a mixture of whole class and individual work but it is the idea of setting or streaming that is attracting more attention. For the harassed teacher struggling to deal with a large class of 30 or more mixed ability children it has a certain appeal. With all pupils at roughly the same stage of development, teaching can be more focused, more uniform in its approach. The planning of lessons becomes more straightforward because there is less need for differentiated activities. If only it was that simple. Any teacher with experience of setting or streaming will know that one could continue to differentiate even within a high ability group of the brightest children. For the truth is that every child's learning needs are unique. Each individual has their own learning style, their own strategies for problem-solving and their own measure of success. Any system for setting or grouping children needs to take this into account if it is to be successful. A point echoed by OFSTED (op. cit.):

> In all cases, the aim must be to provide accurate match between teaching and the abilities and learning needs of pupils by use of appropriate grouping arrangements and by establishing a range of tasks and expectations. Where pupils are taught in ability groups or sets for certain subjects, the school should consider whether;
>
> - the planned provision for different groups or sets matches the range of need in each;
> - the placing of pupils in groups or sets for a given subject is based on valid evidence of ability in that subject;
> - pupils can move easily between groups or sets if their progress indicates this to be appropriate;
> - the curriculum for each group or set is equally well planned and resourced;
> - the effectiveness of setting arrangements is regularly reviewed.

Before attempting to group children in any way within their classroom it is clear that teachers need to ask themselves a number of very important questions. What purpose will it serve? How do you decide what the groupings should be? Should they always be the same? Do children need to be taught specific skills for group-work? In this chapter I will explore the implications behind each of these questions and attempt to offer some practical strategies for developing effective group-work that meets individual needs.

What purpose will it serve?

There are many occasions when children need to work as a group rather than as individuals; for example, when they are involved in team sports, or putting together a play for assembly with everyone taking on a different role. However, even problem-solving activities that could be tackled by an individual may be completed far more efficiently by a group working together, sharing ideas and strategies. Teachers often have their own personal experience of this. More and more schools encourage staff to plan the curriculum together, designing and sharing activities, defining learning objectives and identifying assessment opportunities. In this way teachers do not feel they are overburdened with work, having to come up with all the ideas themselves, 're-inventing the wheel'. I once heard someone jokingly describe teachers as having a 'Burglar Bill' mentality: watch any group of teachers walking around another school, looking at the displays in the classrooms and taking in other people's ideas. You can almost hear them saying to themselves: 'I'll have that!' This is nothing more than the sharing of good practice. Children learn from one another in the same way. Adults often assume that they only pick up bad habits from their peers but with careful organisation of working groups children can pick up positive traits from others in the class. Teachers sometimes move children with behaviour problems around in their classrooms in the hope that they will be influenced by particular role models. Group-work can be used in the same way to share effective working practices.

When children work together as a group they have to communicate with one another; this creates a perfect opportunity for developing speaking and listening skills. They are learning to communicate with different audiences, to be aware of others and to appreciate someone else's point of view. They are often putting forward a hypothesis of their own, thinking out loud and arguing their case: skills absolutely vital for the development of Attainment Target 1 in both mathematics and science and far more likely to occur in a group situation. Of course the teacher needs to be aware that the structure of the group will dramatically affect how well these skills can develop. A quiet, reticent child who is in a group of confident, articulate peers is unlikely to feel encouraged to put forward a point of view that is different from those around him. There will be occasions, however, when that child may well have vital information to offer. Without the 'supportive environment' being put very carefully into place by the teacher his contribution will be lost.

When children are involved in any activity which requires concerted action they need to co-operate. This is an important social skill which most, if not all, teachers would value very highly. But activities of this kind need to be very carefully structured if they are to ensure that all parties contribute equally. By knowing her children, their relative strengths and weaknesses, a teacher can put together groups which contain a wide range of skills and knowledge that can be combined to produce imaginative and effective solutions to a problem.

How will you decide what the groupings should be?

When individuals are assigned to different groups for particular activities it needs to be done on the basis of accurate assessment. You could rely on the outcomes of standardised tests or devise some of your own. The problem is that you might not be asking the right questions.

Many teachers give children an opportunity to show what they already know about a particular topic before they begin work on it. With younger children this can be done orally through group or class discussions but the example on

Egyptian history (*see* Figure 4.1) is a good illustration of how it could be done more formally. This child is already quite an expert on the subject! Concept-mapping (Figure 4.2) is another quick and easy way of conducting initial assessments with children before embarking on a topic. Children simply brainstorm the ideas they have about a particular subject and make links where appropriate. Both these methods of assessment are popular with teachers who have used them because they give immediate insights into the level of development of each individual child. Children like them because they don't require too much in the way of formal presentation. If the exercise is repeated at the end of the topic (e.g. 'What I now know about Egypt'), the information can provide teachers, children and parents with evidence of progress which is accessible and not couched in National Curriculum jargon. The timing of such activities is obviously crucial if they are to influence the teacher's planning. They are most successfully done at the end of the term preceding the particular topic to be studied.

Teachers often express anxiety that the outcomes of such assessments will inevitably lead to widespread differentiation, almost a totally individualised curriculum. In practice most teachers who use such a system report that you actually end up being able to group children into roughly three groups:

- those who already know a great deal about the topic;
- those who know absolutely nothing;
- those who have some idea but it's a bit woolly! (usually the majority).

What the teacher is then able to do is to differentiate her planning for these groups, taking account of where they already are in their learning.

More able children can be encouraged to share their knowledge and expertise with others. They become, in effect, a 'living resource' and can be used to 'tutor' other children. Their self-esteem is enhanced because they feel their knowledge is being valued. Imagine a different scenario. The girl who produced the 'Tudors and Stuarts' example is not given an opportunity to demonstrate what she already knows. The teacher assumes she knows nothing and runs through the basic factual information surrounding Henry VIII. As the days go by she becomes bored and switches off. History (at least as it is taught in school) holds no interest for her.

Children who have difficulty with writing do not have to be excluded from this process if a format is developed which allows them to communicate their knowledge in another way. Many teachers using this system encourage their children to communicate through pictures. The example of the map of Europe (Figure 4.3) could be used in this way. Some children might want to write in the names of countries, capital cities, rivers, mountains, etc., whereas others could simply draw in any famous buildings they are familiar with, national costumes, football shirts, regional food and drink, etc. One Reception class I visited were involved in a topic on 'Water'. Their teacher began by asking them

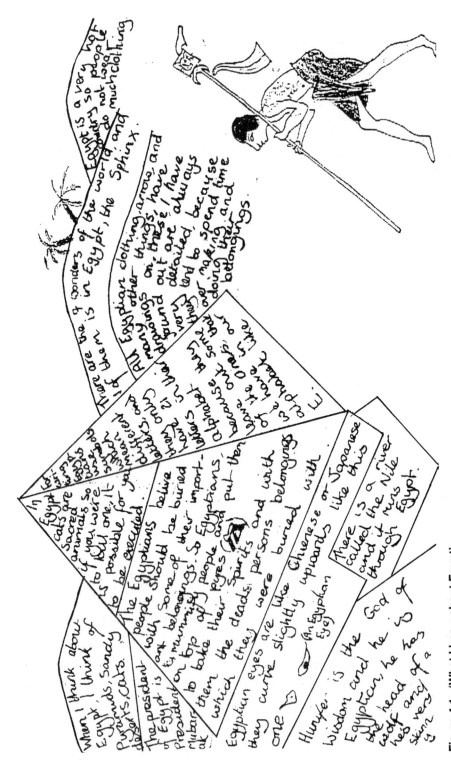

Figure 4.1: 'What I know about Egypt'

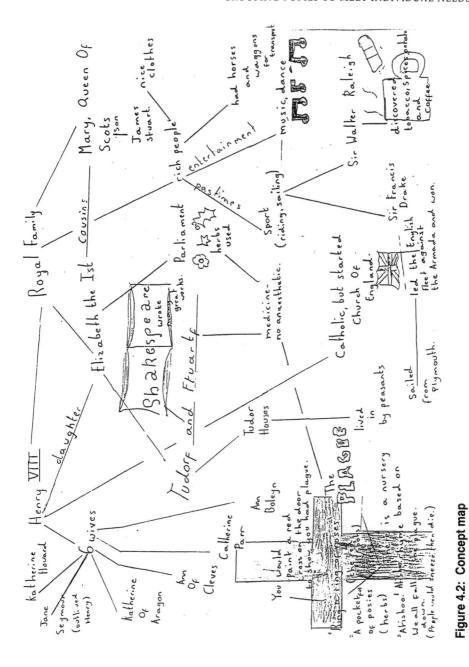

Figure 4.2: Concept map

what they already knew about the way water got into their houses. She asked them to draw their ideas. Some children drew pictures of their parents going out into the street at night, collecting water from a tap or a stream and pouring

Figure 4.3: 'What I know about Europe'

it into a tank in the loft! Others produced detailed diagrams which showed the elaborate system of underground pipes which feed into every house.

The 'Earth' example (Figure 4.4) demonstrates how a teacher can very specifically pinpoint an area of weakness that needs to be worked on. The child has correctly linked ideas about erosion but seems to be rather confused about the relationship between earthquakes and volcanoes!

Once the teacher has this prior knowledge about the level of the children's understanding what does she do with it? Does she automatically group together pupils of similar ability? That is one possibility but there are others. If the 'Earth' child were to be put with a group who knew very little about the

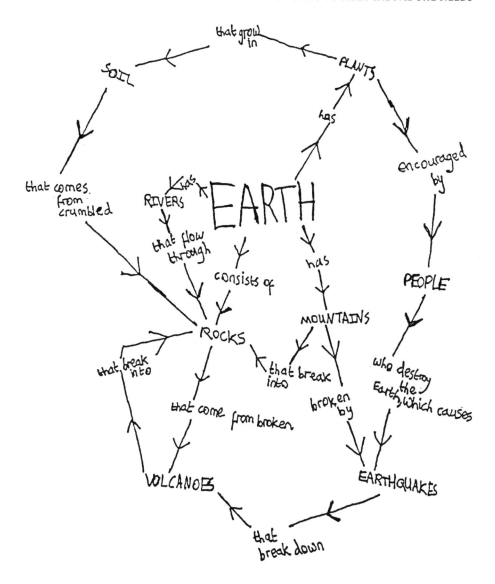

Figure 4.4: 'What I know about the Earth'

subject and asked to explain the links he might well come to understand what is wrong with his logic. Other children would certainly benefit from the 'Tudors and Stuarts' child taking on a 'teaching' role. As with all aspects of planning, the teacher needs to be clear about her objectives for each group.

For experimental science work there is very little point in putting together a group of children who all basically have the same ideas about how an investigation will turn out. If they have similar expectations and make the same predictions then they will have no need to argue for a particular hypothesis.

Should the groups always be the same?

Teachers need to be aware of the danger of children adopting stereotypical roles within a group, particularly if it is well established or the pupils have some control of its membership. 'We've got Susan in our group 'cos she's good at art, she does all the pictures.' Susan's art-work may well improve as a result of this but the development of other skills could be neglected. Teachers need to ensure that children are occasionally faced with unfamiliar and challenging roles.

There is value in getting the children themselves to think about the roles they adopt within a group. Are they typically the organisers or the supporters? Movers or blockers? They can be posed questions that help them become more 'self-conscious' participants. The teacher can organise groups so that pupils are encouraged to take on different roles. Occasionally children could be asked to review the roles they or others took and think about the effect this had on the group dynamics. They could be asked to set themselves targets for future group-work. This is all part of the process of self-assessment. None of this will be possible if the right 'social climate' does not exist in the classroom. If competition is seen as the most important aspect of classroom life then children will not be convinced of the benefits of working together. Group solutions must be seen as valuable. There is a danger that competition between individuals is replaced by competition between groups. That is another good reason for changing the structure of groups whenever possible. It also encourages children to develop the social skills necessary to be able to work with others, adapting their conversation and presentational styles to take into account other children's different personalities and learning styles.

Those outside the world of education certainly value co-operative group-work skills. Conventional academic success has tended to involve largely solitary study, generally uninterrupted work, concentration on a single subject, much written work and a high analytical ability. By contrast, commercially successful companies tend to value the ability to work with others. They want employees who can cope with constant distractions and work at different levels across different disciplines. Problem-solving and decision-making tends to involve mainly verbal skills.

It is, of course, important that the 'constant distractions' of a classroom are carefully regulated! If the verbal skills being developed revolve entirely around the latest episode of a popular 'soap' then they are unlikely to develop beyond social 'chit-chat'. Conversations should have some purpose and be related to the task in hand. If the children are clear about what is expected of them and, equally important, feel that they are being challenged, then they are much more likely to be focused on the activity itself. It would be unrealistic to expect there to be a total absence of social chat but the composition of each group can be critical. A group of children who are all members of a school sports team may well be more concerned about discussing their tactics for the next match than the science investigation that they are supposed to be engaged in!

Do children need to be taught specific skills for group-work?

Children will not automatically understand the 'ground rules' for effective group-work. If, for example, they all try to speak at once then no one will be heard. Even the most convincing argument will be lost. There are certain conventions which have to be taught and practised.

A constant complaint from teachers is that children 'just don't listen'. The reality is that they are much more likely to listen to the teacher than to one another. From a very early age children learn to 'tune in' to the teacher. They know that the teacher will summarise and clarify what is said by others in the class, so what is the point of listening to the other children? One very important technique that teachers use to change this situation is not to echo every contribution so that pupils are forced to listen to one another. They very quickly learn what the new rules are.

There are many games that can be used to train children to listen to one another. One highly enjoyable example is to ask a child to begin re-telling a very well-known fairy tale. After a few sentences the teacher interrupts with a relevant and very specific question, for example: 'Why was she called Red Riding Hood?' 'How old was she?' 'What sort of fruit did she have in the basket?' 'What was wrong with her granny?'

Other children are invited to ask similar questions and usually need very little encouragement to join in. Of course the unfortunate storyteller doesn't get very far with the story but is adding immense detail to bare bones of the original. The other children are having to listen carefully because otherwise they won't know what sort of questions to ask. The teacher can always ask anyone who doesn't appear to be listening to continue the story from a certain point. That certainly encourages them to become rather more involved. This is the principle behind 'hot seating' where one child begins an imaginary tale of their own but is soon asked to hand over to someone else in the group who must continue the story with the same characters, within the same setting and following on from the previous sequence of events.

Another idea is to give children working in small groups a set of cards with random shapes and symbols on each (Figure 4.5). They are asked to decide

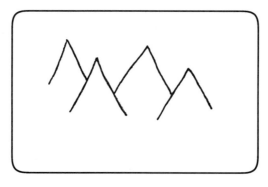

Mountains ?   Shark's teeth ?

Whirlpools ?   Catherine-wheels ?

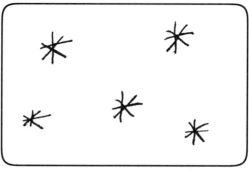

Stars ?   Snowflakes ?

Figure 4.5: Shapes cards

what these could possibly represent and to share their ideas with others in the group. Next they have to try and link these images into a story, eventually presenting them to other children in the class. This activity is ideal for children who find it difficult to come up with ideas for a story or sequence events in any logical way. One school even adapted the idea for a music activity where children were asked to think of the sound that most closely represented their picture.

Another activity designed to help improve and reinforce specific reading skills is to give a small group of children a poem which has been cut up line by line and ask them to reconstruct it. Initially it helps if there is rhyme but children can learn to deal with increasingly more difficult texts surprisingly quickly. They should be encouraged to use clues such as punctuation, the logical sequence of events and later, dialogue.

Children can be asked to give a group presentation of a poem, perhaps illustrated by their own art-work. This may involve different individuals simply reading a line each but children very quickly realise that some lines might require a chorus, or that one character features regularly in the poem and deserves their own 'voice'. Sound effects are particularly appealing to children. It is, of course, very important that the teacher stipulates that all children are involved in the presentation to encourage them all to be involved in the planning and preparation.

I recently came across an example of speaking and listening skills being very effectively developed with a group of six- and seven-year-olds through a history topic. The children had been asked to look at various artefacts and decide a number of things about each one:

- What was it?
- How old was it?
- What was it used for?

In effect they were being asked to hypothesise, justify their opinions with logical arguments and eventually arrive at a consensus view. The activity was given greater impetus because the children knew that they would eventually have to give a formal presentation to the rest of the class explaining why they had arrived at their decision.

Another group of Year 6 children had been involved in a media project which had involved them studying the style and format of various newspapers, ranging from tabloid to broadsheet. In small groups they had to produce their own newspaper within a specified deadline. There was too much material for any one person to deal with so they were forced to share out the work (just as on a real newspaper). Some took responsibility for the sports pages, others for the horoscopes and so on. But it was the follow-up activity which really tested the group's ability to work together as an effective unit. They moved on from newspapers to radio programmes and were asked to mimic the tone and style of their newspaper format. Again a deadline was given which sharpened their focus (and again paralleled the real-life situation). Through simply listening to the tape the teacher was able to monitor the contributions of each individual and assess their progress.

Material developed as part of the National Oracy Project gave some clear and helpful guidelines for the assessment of the skills associated with meaningful talk. In *Teaching, Talking and Learning* (NCC/NOP, 1990) three main areas of development were identified:

- Social skills – how well the group interacts, do they listen to one another? Does one individual tend to dominate? Do they encourage one another to develop ideas, etc.?

- Communication skills – can they present their ideas clearly to an audience?

- Cognitive skills – this is where children are engaged in 'thinking out loud', clarifying for themselves what they mean as they explain it to someone else.

We very often expect children to be able to assess their own progress but this is very difficult if they have not been encouraged to engage in reflective talk. It is important that children have opportunities to discuss personal feelings, celebrate achievement and articulate their hopes and aspirations, but a supportive framework has to be very carefully established within the class-room. The circle-time approaches advocated by Jenny Mosley (1993) and others can be very successful. The teacher timetables occasions when children are able to talk, uninterrupted, about things that concern them. The sessions are quite formally structured, with children taking it in turns to respond to one another and voice their own opinions. The teacher acts as a facilitator, ensuring that order and fair play are maintained, but children very quickly regulate themselves once they are familiar with the process. Circle-time very often involves the whole class but the underlying principles are easily transferred to group-work situations: listening to one another, taking turns, respecting the opinion of others, etc.

Conclusion

The criterion of 'fitness for purpose' should govern teachers' choice of forms of grouping.

(OFSTED, 1996)

There will be occasions when it is more appropriate (and a more efficient use of time) to teach directly to the whole class. Sometimes individual children need to practise particular skills on their own. But it is group-work which best supports the development of oral, social and collaborative skills. Teachers need to be clear what their goals are for each group and to share these with the children. Care needs to be taken with the composition of each group to ensure that all children play an equally important role. This can only be done on the basis of assessment information which takes account of what children already know and understand and uses group-work as a way of developing those areas that need most support. Groups should be flexible units that can be changed and adapted when necessary to suit the learning needs of each individual.

References

Mosley, J. (1993), *Turn Your School Round: Approaches to Circle Time*, LDA.

National Curriculum Council/National Oracy Project (1990), *Teaching, Talking and Learning in Key Stages One and Two*, National Association for the Teaching of English.

OFSTED (1996), *Subjects and Standards: Issues for School Development Arising from OFSTED Inspection Findings 1994–5*, HMSO.

Further reading

Feest, G., Stoate, P. and Thacker, J. (1992), *Group Work Skills: Using Group Work in the Primary Classroom*, Southgate.

Smith, A. (1996), *Accelerated Learning in the Classroom*, Network Educational Press Ltd.

Somerset Education Development Service (1995), *Children's Self Assessment and Self Esteem*, Somerset County Council.

Stanford, G. (1990), *Developing Effective Classroom Groups: A Practical Guide for Teachers*, Acora Books.

5

■ ■ ■

Managing Pupil Behaviour

LAURIE THOMAS

While some schools seem preoccupied with bad behaviour, others have concerted policies for raising expectations and improving standards. The schools we saw which had such positive policies seemed to be very successful in creating an orderly and purposeful atmosphere. They had marginalised bad behaviour by promoting good behaviour.

(DES, 1989)

Behaviour management in schools may be likened to one of the world's most commonly used behaviour management schemes: the Highway Code. Like many road users, school pupils respond well to a positive, well-signposted and commonly accepted series of rules and routines providing order and purpose. To help pupils on their way, rules are supported by both rewards and sanctions, or outcomes. While there are few obvious rewards in the Highway Code there are many powerful outcomes. For the Highway Code to work there must be suitable roads to drive on and somebody to maintain law and order.

As a teacher you work in co-operation with others to design a suitable behaviour code. You design class routines and procedures and ensure that they are kept. Therefore, you are code writer, road builder and police officer. As road builder you seek to construct effective routes into areas of learning and knowledge. Like road builders you recognise your pupils' needs and seek to carry them smoothly on their way.

As traffic police officer you have a responsibility to ensure rules and routines are respected and that the rights of individuals are maintained. When things go wrong you take control and ensure order and smooth flowing. You must know how best to carry out your duties, how to help your pupils take responsibility for their actions and how best to handle those who either cannot control their actions or who purposefully flout rules and regulations.

Finally when behaviour has broken down and pupils are experiencing difficulty coping or re-starting, we need a breakdown service. As classroom AA/RAC agent you need to ensure support is available and on hand when needed.

In this chapter I will give a basic introduction to the construction of a system of classroom behaviour management and the issues of which you – as class teacher – need to be aware. I will work from the premise that you are part of a staff team and that your school has, or is developing, a whole school behaviour management policy. If your school follows a prescribed behaviour management approach such as 'Assertive Discipline' it is important that you first read and follow any guidance already given.

Recent history

There has long been recognition in society of a need for agreed rules and routines and a series of sanctions when these are not adhered to. In past years many rules were followed without an understanding of their importance or value. Sanctions for children were often poorly targeted and – by current standards – overly harsh. The word discipline was often more to do with punishment and retribution than help in managing. If persistently disobedient, children were thought to be possessed of the devil; the preferred treatment was punishment to rid evil spirits or exorcism.

In later more enlightened times using the psychodynamic theory of Sigmund Freud, problem behaviour was identified as originating from within the child's unconscious or subconscious. Garner and Gains (1996) note that such an approach argued that even the earliest experiences of an infant may have an effect on their subsequent behaviour.

The psychodynamicists were road builders; they sought to understand people's needs and help carry them on their way. Their treatments were lengthy and often complex and idiosyncratic. This led many to seek speedier, less ambiguous remedies. By addressing exhibited behaviour rather than guessing at inner needs, learning theorists tried to apply behavioural approaches to people's actions. Such approaches were predicated on the assumption that all behaviour – both good and bad – may be acquired or suppressed. Children may be taught to learn acceptable responses and forget others. Such an approach focused on observed behaviours and outer forces rather than any underlying causation. Behavioural approaches were often imposed on children with little opportunity for negotiation or thought for the context in which behaviours occurred. Opportunities for children to participate in decision making were often minimal. An example of such an approach was the development of *Assertive Discipline* (Canter and Canter, 1976).

The ecosystemic movement recognised that both inner body and outer environmental forces may both affect children. Children were recognised as reacting to their environment and it was noted that the way they reacted to any given situation was the result of interaction between a number of systems. Bronfenbrenner (1979) applied the concept of ecosystems to the study of human behaviour and education. Bronfenbrenner noted how egocentric young children gradually broaden their interactions as they learn and gain confidence. With confidence children integrate into increasingly larger systems as they venture into the world. Problematic behaviour seemed to occur where there was dysfunction between the different systems in which a child interacted. Such an approach encourages teachers to view their pupils' entire situation when addressing a particular behavioural problem. As behaviour managers we look at both a child's needs and how their environment impinges on that child.

Understanding the dynamics

So why do children misbehave?

Our behaviour and the way we interact with the world is a result of many forces both within and around us (Figure 5.1). If our inner self is content and secure we are said to be well adjusted and are capable of coping with considerable change in our external environment (Figure 5.1, point A).

A well-adjusted and secure child will handle and possibly enjoy change. If this child is reared in a non-delinquent environment he feels secure and usually exhibits few behavioural problems. As inner problems and insecurity grow (Figure 5.1, point B) the ability to cope with change in the environment decreases and the likelihood of behaviour problems grows. Such children, while usually settled, may be upset at certain times noticeably on wet and windy days, by changes of routine or unexpected happenings or challenges. A comparison may be made to our own driving. When all is going well and we are driving happily along a road we can take problems such as a delay or long diversion in our stride (Figure 5.1, point A). If we are stressed or late for work such an event may cause upset, possibly invoking uncharacteristic bad language or annoyance (Figure 5.1, point B).

If children's inner problems are greater (Figure 5.1, point C) as a result of trauma, sickness or other serious concerns, their ability to cope with change in their environment further decreases (Figure 5.1, point C). These children may need special approaches and routines to help keep calm and cope with their environment.

Behaviour is generally at its best when children are calm, secure and relaxed (Figure 5.1, point A). While it is not easy to address children's inner forces and subconscious, we can do a great deal to affect the environment that surrounds them. By enabling stimulation, confidence and success we seek to keep a child

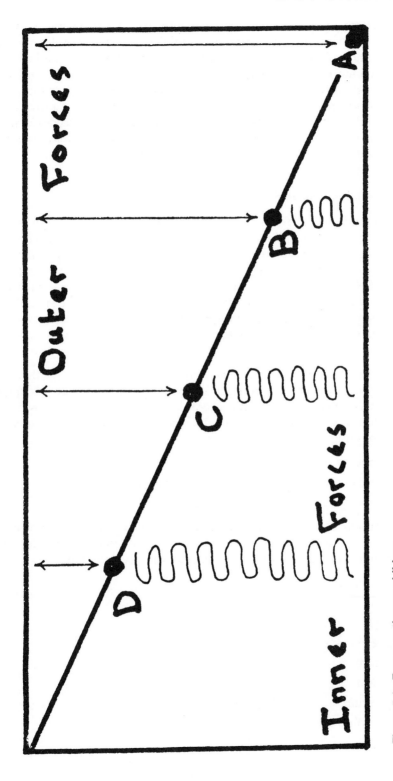

Figure 5.1: Forces acting on children

from travelling up the gradient of inner insecurity towards an area where behaviour problems are more likely. If a child misbehaves, we should apply strategies that provide security, so bringing the child down the gradient away from behaviour problems. Such an approach sounds simplistic and often represents action we least feel like implementing, but such actions underpin much of behaviour management. Security and confidence are provided by using carefully set and consistently applied boundaries, procedures, rules, rewards and sanctions. Children from delinquent backgrounds may need extra help adapting to an agreed and shared value system.

What needs to be done?

Emotional and/or behavioural difficulty (EBD) is a category of special educational need (SEN). While it is highly prevalent in our schools currently, there is no agreed definition (Cooper, 1996). For many, EBD as a special need is seen to lie on a continuum between challenging behaviours within expected bounds to behaviours indicative of serious mental illness. Physical disabilities are generally non-threatening because we can easily identify the special need and understand what help is required. EBD pupils may be threatening to many people because few visual signs identify their needs and their actions may be intimidating.

Left to their own devices an increasing minority of children manage their own behaviour in a manner that threatens safety and restrict the rights of others. While not wishing to enact Golding's *Lord of the Flies* on a daily basis, we carry a professional responsibility as teachers to protect certain rights of pupils and staff by providing an environment where:

- children feel free to learn in safety;
- children can make best use of their learning environment;
- we – as teachers – can work unhindered.

The prevention of behavioural difficulties is of primary importance in the maintenance of a positive learning environment for all pupils. It provides ease of management and more importantly enables the development of:

- on task learning;
- personal accountability;
- respect for others;
- owning of one's own actions;
- self-control;
- self-esteem;
- co-operation;
- safety and protection.

Rules, boundaries and the development of a highway code

Imagine a road system where you may drive on whichever side of the road you please, at whatever speed and in whatever manner you choose. Driving would be difficult and, at best, dangerous. Hence our need as drivers for an agreed set of rules and routines.

Rules form an important part of any system of discipline. We need to know where we stand and what is expected of us. From this we fulfil one of our greatest needs, that of security. Boundaries provide security and rules are psychological boundaries. When carefully set and explained, rules help and protect us. When imposed and misunderstood, they annoy and imprison. It is thus important that rules are understood and ideally owned by all who use them otherwise there will be a temptation to challenge or disregard those rules.

Until relatively recently, children were surrounded by the security of a forest of social rules. Few rules were understood and all were to be accepted. In recent times rules have been increasingly questioned and in numerous cases removed in a search for space and freedom. For many children there now exist so few rules that they float aimlessly in a giant insecure open space. The security once provided by rules is all but gone for these children. It is no wonder then that these children should show little respect for the idea of rules, and that they should have great difficulty accepting consequences.

Our task is to work with all children, to provide the security of a workable code of conduct of rules and routines that may be understood and valued and from which pupils may regain their security, confidence and guidance. Our job is to construct, as part of our behavioural management plan, a behavioural highway code.

When writing our highway code we must be aware that teachers are increasingly finding the common causes of insecurity and behaviour problems to be:

- confusion and insecurity;
- lack of clear guidelines;
- low levels of self-esteem and self-worth;
- lack of suitable stimulation;
- inability to cope in a group;
- inability to accept consequences;
- lack of respect for a system;
- a special educational need not being addressed.

This list arose from a 1994 survey of Kent Primary and Special school teachers which confirmed the research findings of Bill Rogers (1994) in Australia.

If we apply this list to the playground we can see why behaviour problems so often occur. Compared to the security of the classroom with its agreed rules and routines, the playground may be viewed as a large empty insecure space. Here boundaries may be few and activities scarce. Children with low levels of self-esteem may be seeking to integrate using skills they have not yet mastered helped by untrained assistants attempting with minimal guidelines to keep order.

Before we get going, here are seven basic ground rules and some tips to help you establish credibility and classroom control:

1 Address the behaviour exhibited and not the child.

2 Beware the 'street cred' front. Many children develop a hard, unruly outer shell for street survival. This image often protects an insecure and possibly frightened inner child. Try to reach that inner child.

3 Think what is causing this child to behave like this. Do not take their actions or words personally.

4 Be consistent in your approach.

5 Remember a teacher cannot be all things to all pupils and should not feel a failure when the need to seek assistance outside of the classroom arises.

6 Positive behaviour is more likely to occur in an environment where pupils are given the opportunity to develop a shared sense of belonging and identity.

7 Follow a behaviour management plan. Remember most children want to be well behaved and for their lessons to be peaceful and successful.

Development of a classroom behaviour management plan

To help you implement your behavioural highway code and establish effective learning and classroom control it is necessary to have a consistent planned strategy involving three types of action:

1 *Preventative action* (road building and maintenance)
   These are actions that help progress, avoid behaviour problems occurring and so maximise pupils' positive and successful classroom experience.

2 *Corrective action* (road traffic police and managers)
   These actions help us to address and minimise problems as and when they occur.

3 *Supportive action* (breakdown services)
   These actions help pupils regain their self-control and get on their way or defuse potentially volatile situations in a planned, coherent and supportive manner.

The manner in which you address each type of action will be affected by your agreed school policy, your own individual teaching styles, behaviour management skills and daily classroom routines. Here are some ideas that may be of use for the development of your own classroom plan.

Your role as a road builder

These are preventative strategies which will help you carry your pupils smoothly on their way. They may be familiar to you as *'differentiation'*. You seek to prevent behaviour problems from ever occurring, like a good road builder you prevent or remove potential areas of tension, insecurity or conflict. Strategies are required that build smooth roads through the various environments within which pupils travel.

The classroom as a learning environment

Our aim must always be to promote optimum pupil participation, learning and co-operation by effective classroom organisation and layout. To ensure the best chances of good behaviour you must ask yourself the following questions at the start of each session:

Physical layout (road building)

- Do I have an appropriate seating layout or will it encourage behaviour problems?
- Do I have appropriate materials ready to hand and are class resources accessible to all pupils?
- Do I cater for individuals and their special needs?
- Is my classroom a welcoming, aesthetically pleasing and stimulating environment?
- Do I ensure a smooth and clearly understood transition from one activity to another?
- Have I given clear and sensible instructions or have I left pupils in a muddle?
- Does the physical arrangement of my classroom allow various methods of instruction?
- Have I established specific study areas within the room?
- Finally, have I minimised non-essential and distracting stimuli? Will pupils be distracted from their work by other activities or displays?

Rules and Routines (class highway code)

Remember that rules written in the positive form remind us of what to do while rules written in the negative remind us only of what not to do. *'No Running'* is better stated as *'We Walk Slowly'* and *'No Shouting'* is much more effective as *'We Speak Quietly'*.

- Have we as a class constructed a clear set of four or five agreed and published classroom rules or a code of conduct, and are there agreed outcomes?

Class Rules	Class Agreement
1.	If we break the
2.	rules we will:
3.	_____
4.	agreed by:

- Have I established a clearly understood and practised daily weekly routine of tasks, activities and responsibilities?
- Have I defined clear limits for classroom behaviour and academic expectations?

When developing a classroom discipline plan, Alison Moon (1987) suggests you work in consultation with your class and that you state rules positively and explain/discuss the reasons for the rule and the logical consequences of breaking it. Moon also highlights the importance of building on desired behaviours by acknowledging positive actions.

The curriculum and teaching environment

When teaching, the following techniques have been found to help limit misbehaviour by raising pupil awareness, security and success.

Differentiation (road building)

- Be familiar with and adapt if necessary, curriculum guidelines to increase access, understanding and success.
- Clearly define long- and short-term class goals so that we may all know why we are here and where we are going. We also need to know what each of us can expect to get from this change and what each will be expected to give.
- Inform pupils of the daily programme of tasks and activities.
- Explain what pupils will be doing and why.
- Employ a varied programme of instructional approaches, techniques and materials.
- After a careful introduction move quickly into the lesson to minimise the potential for disruption.
- Where possible demonstrate specific activities to show visual and practical value and relevance.
- Ensure that the length and complexity of instructions and tasks are suitable to pupil ability.

Support (road building)

- Be available and accessible to your pupils.
- Provide ongoing feedback, support and exchange of ideas between teacher and pupils.

- Utilise knowledge and enthusiasm of pupils' hobbies and outside interests to bring extra confidence and motivation.
- Know when and how to access help and support to pupils with special educational needs.
- Develop a hierarchy of rewards to recognise effort and on-task behaviour and consequences that are meaningful to pupils and in line with a whole school programme. These should be applied consistently and where possible corporately.

Home–school links

Effective communication between home and school can do much to prevent behavioural difficulties from escalating. Many parents are insecure and frightened that their child may be failing. The following will help raise parental confidence and security and develop consistency between home and school.

Communications (road building)

- Use diplomacy when dealing with parents and adopt a non-threatening and respectful manner.
- Try to build from the positive to the negative. Stress the shared responsibility of home and school and seek to build co-operation and trust.
- Start and finish where possible on a positive note.
- Contact parents when things are going well, not just when problems occur.
- Show appreciation when parents support school.
- Show interest and concern in their child and seek parent or carer views and perceptions.
- State clearly the purpose of any contact and be as specific as possible without being judgemental.
- Focus on one or two issues, provide evidence or documentation and say what has been done to date.
- Seek parental help in addressing and resolving an issue.
- Ensure a degree of privacy and do not infer that the parents are to blame unless there is a clear matter to be addressed. If parents are purposefully breaching school rules be firm, explain the reason for rules and keep to agreed procedures.
- Be aware that some parents may seek to thrust upon you the role of social worker or willing recipient of their every woe. Be ready to refer such parents on to a higher authority.

Your role as a police officer

The development of *corrective action* is an important element in your behaviour management plan. We aim to develop and maintain good behaviour, self-control and a positive environment, however even the most capable of teachers experience behaviour problems within their classrooms. Experienced teachers know that such incidents may be quickly and easily dealt with as long as the correct approach is used. What then should you do and how – in a planned and orderly way – should you address such a situation?

Corrective action consists of a series of pre-planned responses, each designed for children at different levels of misbehaviour. Each response is devised to place responsibility for control on to the pupils' shoulders and hopefully return them to the task at hand. The final response involves support from other staff members and the temporary removal of a pupil from class until they have calmed and the matter may be properly addressed.

A planned approach to behaviour management will help you address all behavioural situations. Here is an example of a planned four-step behavioural approach:

Step one: The giving of a simple direction to return a pupil to task.

Step two: Returning a pupil to task by questioning WHAT (not why) they are doing, and stating a class or school rule.

Step three: If misbehaviour continues give a choice between conformity or sanctions and follow through.

Step four: When faced with highly disruptive, aggressive or dangerous behaviour temporarily remove a pupil from the environment using an agreed exit procedure.

Step one

At its lowest level a pupil's misbehaviour may be to seek attention especially from you as teacher. You may decide to tactically ignore such attention seeking and give attention only when the pupil is on task. Such pupils may be guided back on task by your showing interest in their work, eye contact or any number of agreed visual cues. Aim to keep disruption to a minimum.

If low level guidance is not working then politely and firmly order the pupil to return to his task: 'Back to work please Michael'. Keep your guidance simple and non-confrontational.

Once a pupil has returned to their work, seek to reinforce compliance by acknowledgement of on-task behaviour. Seek to enable pupil satisfaction, attention and success from on-task rather than off-task activity.

While you are directing a pupil they may seek to argue. In this instance, having given a direction, then seek to hinder communication by breaking eye contact or bodily turning away. If a pupil does not stop arguing move to the next level of intervention – Step two.

Step two

Things have not settled. I have one or more pupils misbehaving, what should I now do?

First, think about yourself. Keep calm, do not clench your fists, breathe fast or speed up your voice. Show through your body language that you are unruffled and in full control. Take a slow deep breath, speak slowly and forcefully and try the following:

If a child continues to misbehave or argue, break this disruptive cycle by asking the question 'What should you be doing'.

At all times maintain eye contact. Minimise embarrassment with a respectful tone of voice that suggests you are calm, in perfect control and mean business. If a pupil does not tell you what he should be doing give him time to do so or save face, then you may re-state the rule.

Do not enter into discussions about other secondary issues. These will be red herrings introduced as a diversionary tactic to move you away from the primary misbehaviour. For example:

'Wayne, please sit down.'

'But Tracey is lending me her pen!'

'What should you be doing Wayne?'

'I'm getting a pen that Tracey lent me. Didn't you Tracey?'

'What should you be doing? You should be sitting down in your place. On you get.'

If a pupil starts to argue you may re-state a rule or direction about a primary issue repetitively word for word rather than argue a secondary issue. Ensure that your words remain clear and calm, speak slowly and maintain eye contact.

Give power to your words by pausing before certain key words. When the pupil conforms say thank you. Build on any opportunities for success by complimenting once a pupil is back on task and working well.

Step three

If a child continues to misbehave it is important we make them responsible for their own actions. Give the pupil a choice to behave or receive a sanction, such as moving away to work on their own. It is important if the pupil does not behave that they receive an effective sanction. If the child chooses the sanction so be it, ensure that such a sanction bites.

An effective sanction for stage three pupils may be (space permitting) to physically isolate a pupil within the classroom. Being one of the class becomes an honour to be earned. They must now seek their way by good behaviour back into the class group. Such a strategy should show class members such behaviour is not tolerated. This strategy may also give pupils a welcome break from the antics of a tiresome class member.

Upon further misbehaviour pupils must understand there is a hierarchy of sanctions; that whatever their actions there will be a response and they will have to pay the appropriate penalty unless they agree to conform.

By providing the security of a boundary of cause and effect, extra strength will be provided, especially to the insecure child who may well be used to a passive management style of moving boundaries and forgotten sanctions. Such children may repeatedly challenge authority, not to cause upset but to ensure that the boundaries provided remain solid and secure.

For effective behaviour management it is necessary to keep to your word, however difficult it may be. As long as you are seen to be fair and consistent you will be respected. Deviate or give way and although you may think you are viewed as kind to pupils, you will be seen as ineffective; an easy pushover.

More importantly you will have shown to your class that the boundaries you give provide little security. You will have built the equivalent of a weak and wobbly fence to secure your garden. If a fence is weak and wobbly we shake it to see just how secure it might be. If it wobbles badly we shake harder to ascertain its strength. If it is really loose, we knock the fence down and start again. These are the actions of insecure pupils faced with a weak teacher.

If you have been a passive or insecure disciplinarian, it is quite easy to firm up your boundaries. But do not be surprised if pupils try repeatedly to misbehave to check if you mean business. Remember the fence must not wobble no matter how many times your pupils seek to shake it!

Step four

This step is about an agreed exit procedure.

If pupil behaviour reaches a point where it becomes dangerous, aggressive or where it seriously disrupts learning within the group, it is important that an offending pupil or pupils be temporarily removed from that situation. To remove pupils effectively, it is important that school staff, as part of their behaviour management plan, develop an agreed school exit procedure.

A carefully and corporately developed exit procedure will provide security to both staff and pupils. Staff will know that whatever a pupil's behaviour, there will always be a planned school response. Staff will have a procedure to call upon should they require assistance. Pupils will know that their behaviour can be managed and that school rules and behavioural boundaries will stand firm regardless of their actions. An exit procedure requires three things:

- co-operation and teamwork from all staff;
- a system of quick adult response and support;
- a named adult capable of taking offenders for temporary respite.

If a pupil requires removal a message will be sent to a particular member of the staff team (some schools send a red card) and a planned course of response activated. Once summoned, a teacher will seek to remove the offending pupil causing minimal disruption and upset. Once removed the pupil will be taken to another setting where they will be expected to continue their studies. At the first opportunity the pupil will meet with their teacher who will address the matter.

If a pupil seeks to challenge the school's behaviour management system and refuses to leave their class, the class members will de-camp with their teacher to another location leaving the pupil and exit teacher, and so calling the offending pupil's bluff. Having challenged the behavioural boundaries and found them to be firm, most pupils can be easily removed to another location and the class returned to their room. Although disruptive, such action does not need to be repeated too often as word soon spreads of its effectiveness.

If more than a few pupils are involved or if the level of risk is high, it may be safest to seek wider support from senior management and follow their advice. At all times priority must be given to the safety and welfare of pupils and staff.

Teachers are entitled to support when teaching children and young people with difficult or unusual behaviour.

(NUT, 1996)

If exit procedure does not work or is used more than once for any one pupil, the matter must be referred to your headteacher or a senior member of staff and the school Special Educational Needs Co-ordinator for further consideration of the child's programme, special needs and placement. A record should also be kept of pupils reaching steps three and four of the behaviour management plan. Remember:

- It is the behaviour and not the pupil's personality that should be addressed.
- Recognise that increased security will help calm a situation while increased insecurity may fan the smallest upset to a potentially explosive situation.
- At all times seek to repair and build on the positive.

So how should I discipline a child?

'*It ain't what you do but the way that you do it.*'

Bill Rogers (1994) identifies thirteen protocols of discipline which, if followed, greatly assist the teacher when correcting pupil behaviour. While not wanting to reiterate this list it is important that in our interaction with pupils we are aware of the dynamics of the situation and how these may help or hinder the situation we seek to address.

Establish clearly the rights, rules and responsibilities of your class as discussed earlier. If breached it may be best to discipline disruptive pupils away from the peer group. If the peer group are present a pupil may seek to maintain his street cred image by playing to the gallery. In this situation the pupil will be giving more thought to his audience than to what you may or may not be saying. At all times it is important to ensure pupils are given the opportunity to take responsibility for their own behaviour.

Treat pupils as you would like to be treated. As a role model, set and maintain high standards. Be aware that our expectations affect our behaviour as classroom leaders. Also if reprimanding a pupil it is important to be seen to carry the matter through.

Seek where possible to build bridges with a child's parents and peers. A useful tool for behaviour management is an effective working relationship. Be seen to work closely with fellow staff and parents to ensure help and a consistency of approach.

When disciplining a pupil, their response will have much to do with how they perceive your emotional state and your behaviour towards them. Pupils will seek to read your body language and one of the most powerful indicators will be the nature and tone of your voice. Keep a pupil calm and secure through careful, assertive use of your voice. Slow your speech, lower your pitch, speak clearly and add power to your words by putting a wait time after key words.

'What/ /did I tell you to do/ /Wayne?'

Watch your proximity to a pupil. We all possess a personal body space. For an adult to invade this space may heighten insecurity and so fuel upset and misbehaviour. Pupils should, however, be asked to maintain eye contact except where culturally it is bad manners to do so.

Avoid arguing as this will distract pupils from on-task behaviour and may escalate into a more serious incident. Be assertive from the start and if necessary follow your behaviour management plan. Make reference to the agreed and clearly posted class rules which are there to help pupils own their own behaviour and respect the rights of others.

Always seek to use the minimum assertion necessary, this will save your energy levels and blood pressure, reduce class disruption and leave greater assertion in hand for any higher levels of disruption.

I once entered a room ranting and raving to reprimand a pupil for a relatively minor offence. My rationale was to send a powerful short sharp shock to my class pupils saying 'This teacher should not be meddled with'. After my tirade had subsided – with me still shaking and red in the face – the pupil quietly looked me in the eye and calmly said 'What are you going to do next time, kill me?'

Finally, and most importantly, once settled in, seek to maintain a judicious sense of humour in your everyday class management. School and learning should be fun. The use of humour provides body language suggesting all is well, that the user is relaxed, secure and content and likes their company. Certainly it is not easy to use humour effectively if you are feeling tense or insecure. However humour can often be used to defuse all but the most tense situations.

For further help and guidance I strongly recommend the work of Bill Rogers.

What about a breakdown service?

This is the provision of *supportive action* if pupils break down.

Following behaviour breakdown, it is important that both pupils and staff be supported. It is vital that the responsibility for behaviour is accepted as a teaching problem. Children exhibiting emotional and/or behavioural difficulties may require individual educational programmes containing effective behavioural management programmes and it will be important to involve pupils in the setting of behaviour targets and drawing up of any contracts.

There is a need for meticulous follow-up action after corrective discipline. When a pupil is calm then talk through and act out incidents, discuss alternative responses and, where helpful, introduce relevant social skills. Many pupils are able to construct helpful coping strategies and these need to be agreed with the pupils concerned. Many pupils also appreciate the opportunity to make amends and rebuild. Explain why the consequences were applied, how the matter may be put right and how to re-establish a good working relationship.

As teachers we need to develop good listening skills and know who to approach to access suitable counselling support. It is important that we understand school procedures for conferencing and contracting with both pupils and parents. We must similarly understand the nature and limits of staff support for behavioural and pastoral issues and child protection procedures when necessary.

Conclusion

So that's it. You now have a growing idea of the pupils' needs and with their help you are constructing a network of differentiated and clearly signposted educational roads, route ways and rules to help carry them on their way.

As part of your written code of conduct (or highway code) you will hopefully develop a system of meaningful rewards and sanctions to help enable smooth traffic flow and the development of self-control.

To ensure your highway code is adhered to you will have developed a system of planned responses. You will have understood how best to interact with your road users and have to hand an effective breakdown and support service. Finally you will, with pupil help, regularly inspect the condition of your roads and fill in any potential potholes.

Good luck!

References

Bronfenbrenner, U. (1979), *The Ecology of Human Development*, Harvard University Press.

Canter, L. and Canter, M. (1976), *Assertive Discipline: A Take Charge Approach for Today's Education*, Lee Canter Associates.

Cooper, P. (1996), 'Giving it a name: The value of descriptive categories in educational approaches to emotional and behavioural difficulties', *British Journal of Learning Support* **11(4)**.

Department of Education and Science (1989), *Discipline in Schools: Report of the Committee of Enquiry into Discipline in Schools (The Elton Report)*, HMSO.

Garner, P. and Gains, C. (1996), 'Models of intervention for children with emotional and behavioural difficulties', *British Journal of Learning Support* **11(4)**.

Moon, A. (1987), *Skills For The Primary School Child*, TACADE.

National Union of Teachers (1996), *Discipline in Schools*, NUT.

Rogers, W.A. (1994), *Behaviour Recovery*, Longman.

Further reading

Rogers, Bill (1994), *Managing Behaviour Series: Positive Correction, Consequences, Prevention, Repair and Rebuild: Four Videos Dealing with Positive Discipline and Classroom Management*, Quartus.

6

■ ■ ■

Managing the Classroom Environment

JULIE BRIANT

In order to meet the educational and emotional needs of pupils it is important to plan an effective learning environment where there is a positive ethos for learning, a common sense of purpose, where children feel safe and secure and are confident enough to take risks.

The way the classroom is organised does impact on how children are taught, how they behave, how they learn and the standards they achieve. The desirable outcomes for children's learning on entering compulsory education and the National Curriculum place emphasis on pupils being enabled to make choices and decisions in relation to their work and to be involved in problem-solving activities.

Children and adults have to feel comfortable in the working environment, there has to be a sense of ownership by all who use the classroom and the rules of how to use the room need to be clearly understood.

If we as teachers are to enable children to achieve high standards, what is it that we have to do? We need to create a classroom where the processes of learning are developed and where children are given time and space to develop their thoughts.

There are common threads of effective classroom management that run through reception, Key Stage 1 and Key Stage 2 but there are also differences.

The use of space

There will never be enough space in any classroom and many have inappropriate furniture and inadequate display space. What is important is that you make the most effective learning environment with what you have already in place. If you have an open-plan classroom the difficulty may be too much space and the management of a shared creative area with another teacher. The use of a shared area has to be carefully negotiated and standards for tidiness and expectations of pupils have to be agreed at the start of the partnership.

The creative or wet area may already be clearly defined by tiling on the floor and the siting of the sink. The quiet area may be the only place in the classroom that has a small piece of carpet. There may be limited electric points. Display boards may be sited in inappropriate places. So, you may have to look at the fixed areas and decide how best they can be used and then focus on the remaining space which can be used more flexibly. You will have to make the decision early on if every child will need a chair and a place at a table in the classroom or if you want children to move around and work at different areas during the course of the day. Stools take up less space and can be positioned at benches for children to work at. If children are not given fixed places, they will need somewhere to keep their personal belongings, for example trays under benches.

Do you as a teacher need a desk? In many classrooms the teacher rarely sits at her desk and it can take up valuable space. It often becomes the dumping ground for everything and anything. The desk itself is rarely seen! If you decide not to have a desk you will need somewhere to keep your papers, files, etc. These can be stored safely on a shelf or in a filing cabinet. Children should be taught to respect the areas in the classroom where adults store their personal and private belongings.

Classrooms sometimes become cluttered with things that may become useful. As a teacher it is very difficult to throw things away but it is important to be ruthless at times and to only have in the classroom what is really of use to you and the children. But, before you throw away anything do check with the appropriate curriculum co-ordinator to ensure that items are not needed by another teacher later in the year. If these resources are needed later then place them in the main storage areas in the school.

If working areas are established you have to make sure that all children have access to them during the day otherwise parts of the classroom will be under used. An effective environment is one that is used by pupils and adults in a purposeful way throughout the whole day. To negotiate with pupils at the beginning of the year where they think working areas, materials and tools could be positioned is an effective way to ensure that children have ownership of the room and that they know where everything is. They often see the classroom in a better light as they are the ones using it. They will often tell the teacher how difficult it is to work in an area because it is cramped or how hard it is to access resources easily. Children can help draw up a plan of the classroom using squared paper. The layout of the room can then be reviewed at an agreed time or when problems occur.

The organisation of space must enable children and adults to move freely around the room and to access tools and materials easily. Vision must be good to all areas of the classroom so that children can be easily supervised and helped where necessary.

Space outside the classroom can be used effectively, some corridors are wide enough to be used for some paired or group work, parts of cloakrooms can be used as working areas and the outside environment can be used successfully, weather permitting. Garden tables and benches sited outside classrooms can be a useful extension to the inside learning environment.

Daily planning will often identify how children will be grouped, where they will work and the resources needed. This is managing the classroom environment on a daily basis. Creating working areas which focus on areas of the curriculum is one effective way of organising children's learning. This suggests that all the resources needed for one aspect of learning can be kept together in one place. Groups of children can then work successfully on different aspects of the curriculum. On occasions where the whole class may be working on one area of the curriculum the layout of the classroom and the organisation of resources will be different. The flexibility of seating and table arrangements for different purposes is an important feature of good classroom management. For some aspects of whole class teaching you may decide to use an overhead projector. It will be important for this activity that the seating is arranged to enable all children to participate in the session effectively.

Daily planning can be shared with pupils. Their tasks and where they are to work can be written on an easel or white board and shared with the children at the beginning of sessions. Other available activities can be clearly stated so that each pupil knows where they are to be working and the tasks they are due to complete.

Access to the computer, the CD ROM and other forms of Information Technology (IT) need to be carefully thought through as does the storage of discs, CDs and overlays for the Concept Keyboard. It is important that IT is used as an everyday tool. The siting of the computer is important. The screen needs to be placed in an appropriate light and the seating and table height need to be correct. This will help children to acquire the right posture for working. There are different ways to organise the use of IT within the classroom. The computer can be placed in the writing area, within a role play area, for example an office, or a separate IT area can be established. The number of children working at the computer needs to be carefully planned. If two children are working together, is one child always the passive partner? Would it be better for one child to have individual access to the computer for some aspects of work?

Working areas can be created by using storage benches, low cupboards and shelving. Small easy chairs can create a quiet reading area and the use of plants can help to create areas and make the classroom a pleasant place to work in. Storage benches and cupboards can be used as display space for artefacts, books, etc. The use of trellising and corrugated card can be used to create small screens and for displaying pupils' work. If the classroom ceilings are low or there are ceiling supports then fabric, netting and paper strips can be used effectively for dividing the room and for displaying work.

Two examples of possible classroom layouts are given in Figures 6.1 and 6.2. Within the classroom environment it is important that children know what they can work on once they have finished a teacher directed task. These tasks need to be worthwhile and challenging. Artefacts or plants can be left in the art area for children to observe closely and draw or paint. Task cards can be left near construction materials, a mathematical challenge can be set up, the book area can be used for quiet reading and the writing area can be used for children to complete extended writing tasks. Within this type of classroom environment children are involved in purposeful activities and not in low-level 'choosing' tasks.

Resources

The effective organisation, maintenance and storage of resources is crucial to the smooth running of any classroom. Resources have to be easily accessible and well labelled. For younger children it is important to have pictures as well as words on the outside of boxes and trays. To help children with the putting away of resources it is useful to have drawn outlines of tools, etc. Children can then match equipment to the correct outline. The number of items in use can be added to the display, for example '5 calculators'. This helps children and adults to check that the correct number have been replaced. Open shelving is preferable to cupboards with doors. Clear routines for tidying up need to be established early on so pupils are aware of your expectations and their role within the activity.

To enable children to work independently and to make their own choices and decisions, the effective organisation of resources is crucial. Children should not have to waste time asking where resources are or if they can use them unsupervised. They should be able to get on with certain tasks on their own enabling the teacher to teach the group she is working with. Caroline Gipps (1992) states that:

> Classrooms should have a shared responsibility for learning: the teacher structures the session and allocates the task, but the child has responsibility for how the task is carried out and has some responsibility for his or her learning, thus reducing dependency on the teacher.

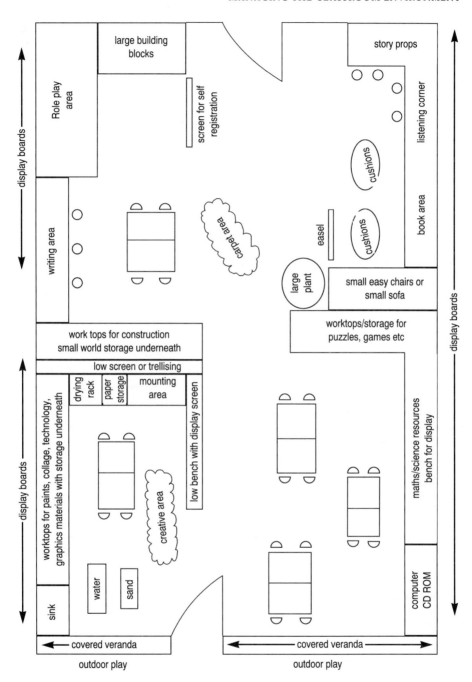

Figure 6.1: Reception and Key Stage 1 – Classroom plan

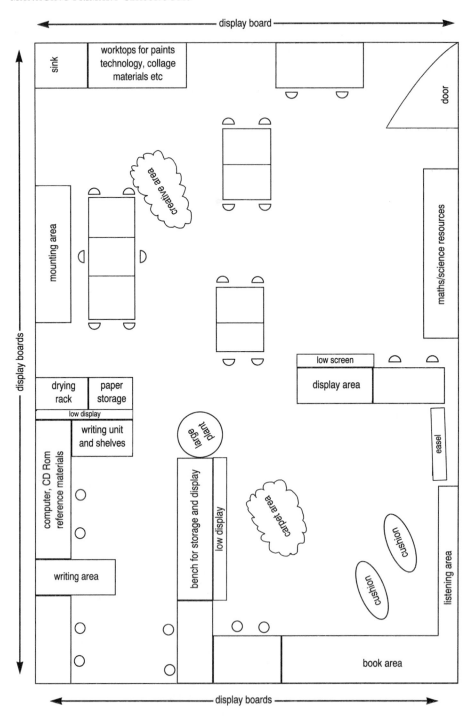

Figure 6.2: Key Stage 2 – Classroom plan

In any class there will be a number of children with special educational need (SEN). Some of these children will need special equipment and resources. It will be important that their resources are easily available to them so they can access them quickly in order to start their work. Pairing of pupils is an effective way to ensure that children with SEN are effectively supported in the classroom.

It is important that children have somewhere to keep their own personal belongings within the classroom. If they have individual trays in storage benches it is sensible to have these clearly labelled and positioned in different parts of the room. This will ease congestion especially at busy times, for example when children start and finish their work.

Many children have book bags which they use to take their reading/story/non-fiction book home in. Storage of these can be difficult as 30 book bags can create a cluttered effect and can cause classroom chaos as they are collected at the beginning and end of each day. Four smaller boxes or baskets for book bags can be positioned in different parts of the room at the beginning and end of the day. This will help to ease congestion. The boxes can be stored in the book corner during the day for children to have access to their own books as necessary.

The choice of storage boxes and containers for resources needs to be considered carefully. The correct size is important so that resources do not look untidy or overspill into the next box or shelf. You need to ensure that the maximum number of boxes fit into the allocated space and children can get them in and out of the unit easily. The weight of the boxes also needs to be considered. Children need to be able to lift them safely. If equipment is heavy it can be stored in a wheeled container. Different colour storage boxes should be used for different types of equipment. This helps children to locate and replace resources easily. Wicker baskets are useful for storage as they make less noise than plastic and the natural colour does not detract from the classroom environment or display. They may, however, need coloured labels on them.

Polythene wallets are good for storing smaller equipment. The wallets enable children to see what is inside and a large number of wallets can be stored in one box or basket.

The storage and organisation of art materials can be difficult. If children are to mix their own paints it is useful to provide a selection of small containers for powder paint and one for water that fit onto a tray. These can be easily carried by children and used without enormous wastage of paint. Palettes need to be available and kept clean by pupils. A selection of brushes needs to be provided so that children can choose the right brush for the task. Sharp implements such as scissors should be safely stored and children need to be clear about the rules for using them.

Tables often look messy covered with newspaper. A PVC cloth provides a washable surface and helps to create a pleasant working area. Children also need to be well covered when undertaking messy activities. To ensure that pupils put on protective clothing it should be positioned in a prominent place and easily available.

Display

The way work is displayed in the classroom is important. It makes a clear statement about the quality of pupils' work, the standards achieved by pupils, what is valued by the teacher and how much ownership of the classroom environment pupils have.

Before work is displayed it is important to think about the background colour schemes. Although it is important for classrooms to be bright and stimulating places, background colour should not fight or detract from the display of pupils' work. The same is true of very ornate and patterned borders. It is worth considering the use of hessian or other natural and subtle fabrics for the backing of display boards. Although this is expensive at the outset it is cost effective and time saving in the long run, as fabric does not have to be replaced as each new display is mounted. The colours used on the display boards in the classroom need to be co-ordinated to help create the right ethos and atmosphere within the room.

Central areas or corners for display can be created by using corrugated card. Artefacts can then be displayed along with children's work. Magnifying glasses and viewing jars should be readily available so that objects can be closely observed. Outlines can again be useful to ensure that the correct number of magnifying glasses are returned at the end of the session. Labels on a display need to inform children about what can be handled and what can just be looked at. They need to be of a uniform style and/or size. Children can hand write or make computer-generated labels.

The use of picture and clip frames to display work is effective. It shows that children's work is valued and gives it status. A picture gallery can be created within the classroom or outside in the corridor as a permanent feature with pictures changed at regular intervals. The children should be involved in choosing the pictures for the gallery.

The use of well-known artists' work to support displays is effective, for example where art and history are being studied together. Where close observational work is displayed it is a good idea to present the object alongside the children's work.

A display of photographs can record achievement in areas of the curriculum that are not undertaken in the classroom, or those areas which are not easily recorded (for example PE, drama, pond work). They can also be used to record first-hand experiences of visits and visitors to the school and can act as an *aide-*

mémoire for children once they have returned to the classroom. The use of photographs to record interesting constructions and structures is useful. Children enjoy remembering what they have built and it can act as a reference point for further work.

The use of different levels for display is visually pleasing. Hessian covered boxes, boxes covered with drapes and small stage plinths can all be used effectively for stands. The use of small plants, vases of flowers and natural objects can also help enhance a display.

Children need to be involved in the planning and making of displays. Even the youngest children can mount their own work; choosing appropriate backing paper and using a paper trimmer to create the right size border. Older pupils can lay out the display, they can choose the colour scheme and eventually be responsible for the whole display. If the first few attempts are not successful a notice can be added to the display informing the observer that this is one of the first attempts made by children to display their own work.

Children should get into the habit of writing their names on all pieces of their work. If younger children need help with this they should be able to access their name cards easily. Small computerised name labels are very useful for placing on models as it is often extremely difficult to write a name on a model made from found materials.

The purpose of the display needs to be decided before the first picture goes onto the wall. It may focus on one theme or on a collection of different types of writing. It may give information, raise questions, or celebrate children's achievement. Once the purpose has been decided the layout can be planned, the size and shape of mounting paper decided and the type of lettering agreed upon. It is important to test the layout of the display by fixing each picture or piece or work with a drawing pin before using the staple gun. This gives you the opportunity to make adjustments to the display as you work on it. It is frustrating if you finish the display to find that the last picture will not fit, or the display is unbalanced.

If the purpose of the display is to give information to children, or to celebrate children's writing, do ensure that it is displayed at a height that children can read and enjoy it. Paintings can be displayed at a higher level and can still be appreciated.

You need to ensure that the quality of adult writing on display is good. It acts as a model for pupils and if it is untidy or uneven it detracts from the quality of the display. Many teachers find large writing difficult. The use of commercially produced letter templates and the use of computer generated large script can help to solve this problem. The placing of the lettering also needs to be carefully considered. The best place is not always at the top of the board. Placing the lettering to one side or in the middle of the display can be more effective. The colouring of the lettering should be chosen to enhance the display not to dominate it. The adult writing used should reflect the school's chosen style. In many cases this involves the use of a full cursive style or the use of entry and exit flicks. A chart of the chosen style of writing should be displayed so that children can refer to it when needed.

If children are to learn effectively and achieve well it is important that it is made explicit what it is that they are expected to learn and whether they have achieved it. As part of the display it is useful to have a chart informing pupils what it is you want them to learn over a stated period of time. As areas are covered they can be marked off with the pupils giving them a sense of achievement and satisfaction in their learning. Alongside can be placed a chart that outlines what they knew about the subject already. This information can be gained through a class brainstorming session or by individual children recording what they already know about the topic. Through this display children gain an understanding of what they know and what they need to learn. If the brainstorming session takes place before planning the new topic, it gives the teacher a chance to adjust the planning so that future work meets children's learning needs.

An area of display can also provide a place for children to keep track of their own achievement. If children are encouraged to review the work they have undertaken they can with the support of the teacher set targets for themselves, record the targets on index cards, place the cards in envelopes and display and review them at regular intervals. This reflection on their learning helps them to see their own progress and to see learning as a whole, not as a series of isolated instances.

Some display board should be given over to children's own messages and should be managed by the pupils. The message board can be sited in the writing area. Children are then near to the writing materials in order to make a reply. A parent's notice board is also useful to display the latest letter from school or to ask for help or resources.

The reception environment

A large number of four-year-old children are now being educated in reception classes. For some children this is their first experience of school. An appropriate classroom environment is therefore very important if the children are to settle and make a positive start to schooling. The curriculum for four-year-olds should be delivered through a well-planned and resourced classroom and outdoor environment. This environment needs to provide a range of educational areas which children can move within and between in order to pursue chosen and directed interests. These areas will include:

- role play;
- book area;
- construction area including a large space for block play;
- creative area to include malleable and technology materials;
- natural materials: sand, water, clay, science investigations;
- writing/graphics area;
- small world area;
- puzzle/mathematical games area;
- outdoor play area.

Within the environment it is important that children can find something familiar to play with as well as finding new and stimulating equipment and materials. Young children often need to play with the same toy or piece of equipment at the beginning of the session. This helps to reassure them that they are in control of this very new experience called school. Free access to resources is therefore vital if children are to make these important choices. It is only when children feel that they have choice and control over what happens to them within the environment that they will begin to learn effectively.

Children can self-register at the beginning of each session by using name cards with Velcro or magnetic strips on the back. This helps them to settle to work, to feel part of the classroom, and gives them an opportunity to recognise their own name and names of other children in the class. It is also a double registration check for the teacher.

A message or question can be written on an easel for the children as they enter the classroom. This encourages parents to read to their children as they enter. If a question is asked, for example 'Did you look at the tadpoles yesterday?' children can write their name under the yes/no column. This information can then be used for early data collection work at group time. A message can help stimulate interest in an area of the room, for example in the role play area: 'Goldilocks has left a message for the Three Bears in their house. I wonder what it says?'

Within the book area it is useful to have a selection of story books with props in polythene wallets. These props help children to retell the story using concrete objects. They also help encourage those children who are reluctant to sit down and read a book. The placing of a tape recorder/listening centre in the book corner with taped stories is another way to encourage children to sit and listen to a story. A storage box for pupils' reading records should be placed in the book area. This gives staff easy access to records.

Clip boards placed in the construction area encourage children to draw what they have made. These drawings can be used to extend or recreate the structure, or can act as a plan for another child.

The outdoor environment needs to be carefully managed and planned. It should link effectively with the indoor learning environment, for example, outside role play areas such as garden centres and garages can include writing materials, calculators, etc. Timers can be used for turns on bikes and trucks; bikes can have numbers on them to correspond with numbers on the wall for parking. This helps children to develop their understanding of mathematics. To help children use writing purposefully, they can sign on a board to show they have had a turn on equipment. A roadway with arrows and signs can be created to help develop geographical understanding and increase knowledge of direction and safety.

Young children in both reception and Key Stage 1 often have the opportunity for a drink of milk or juice. This can be organised so that children help themselves to a drink during the session rather than setting time aside for the whole class to have a drink. Pupils' names can be placed around the drink for easy identification. They can then help themselves when they are thirsty. Pupils will need to know where they can sit to have their drink. It is not safe for them to wander around the classroom with a carton of juice or a bottle of milk.

The Key Stage 1 environment

Much of what has been stated in the section on reception is appropriate for children in Key Stage 1, although the curriculum on offer is based on the requirements of the National Curriculum. Pupils in Key Stage 1 still need to be active learners and they should have access to a wide range of materials that challenge their thinking and learning. Role play areas will need to be more sophisticated. They should offer opportunities for shopping with 'real' money with the computer and printer being used to raise orders and invoices for use in the shop. A coin sheet for matching coins back after use, at the end of the session, should stop them going home in pockets. Pupils can be involved in the designing and setting up of role play areas. Menus and place mats can be designed and printed, and invitations to parties can be issued.

Books for research need to be organised alongside displays so that children can access information for themselves from a variety of sources. CD ROMs also need to be available for research. Key words/word banks will need to be made available to children so they can proceed in their writing independently.

Books in the book corner need to be stored in an agreed way with the children, so they can be clear about how to tidy away at the end of the session. When an author is chosen as a focus all the books by him/her can be displayed together. Children may complete work based on a particular story; this can then be displayed in one area.

The Key Stage 2 environment

There appear to be two types of learning environment in Key Stage 2. For younger children within the key stage the environment is usually managed in the same way as Key Stage 1, and in many primary schools this organisation remains more or less similar for the whole of Key Stage 2. However, in many schools, for older children the learning environment often changes as they are put into sets according to their ability for work in the core subjects of English, mathematics and science. Children may be organised into home bases but for parts of the day may move round to different rooms and be taught by different teachers for different subjects. Some children find this type of organisation difficult to adjust to. It can also be difficult for teachers who have to manage the environment effectively as a home base for children and as a classroom for the teaching of a specific curriculum subject. Within the home base children still need to have a sense of belonging. They should have somewhere to place their personal items where they will not be disturbed by other children using the classroom.

Resources will need to be organised into curriculum areas and placed into appropriate rooms. Tools and materials still need to be easily accessible and a range of different equipment needs to be available so that children can make their own choices and decisions, especially when they are involved in problem-solving activities.

How and where work will be displayed should be decided at an early stage. Is work to be displayed in subjects within subject areas or is it to be displayed in their own home base? How are children's books to be stored? Will they be kept with the teacher who is teaching the subject, or will they all be kept in the children's home base, so that children can access them as they are needed?

How much equipment and resources will be kept in a central area so that children can access it as they need it? If materials are kept in a central store how will children know what is available?

Conclusion

The effective management of the classroom environment is crucial if children are to be fully involved in the processes of learning, if they are to behave appropriately and if they are to achieve high standards. The learning environment needs to be continually reviewed and questioned. Some of the questions that can be asked by all teachers are:

- Is the classroom attractive to children and adults?
- Is it a tidy and comfortable place to work in?
- Do children have a sense of ownership?

- Is space used to the best advantage?
- Is the furniture arranged appropriately for the work being undertaken?
- Can children work and learn independently?
- Are resources and equipment used efficiently and effectively?
- Does the classroom environment enable me to carry out my planned work effectively?
- Are the other areas outside the classroom used effectively?
- Can children start their work quickly?
- Is IT used as an integral part of the classroom?
- Is there room for individual, paired and group work?
- Is the layout appropriate for whole class teaching?
- After children have finished their directed work, do they always have purposeful work to be involved in?

Reference

Gipps, C. (1992), *What We Know About Effective Primary Teaching*, University of London Institute of Education/Tufnell Press.

Further reading

Bull, S.L. and Solity, J.E. (1989), *Classroom Management: Principles to Practice*, Routledge.

Dean, J. (1983), *Organising Learning in the Primary School Classroom*, Routledge.

Edwards, A. and Knight, P. (1996), *Effective Early Years Education: Teaching Young Children*, Open University Press.

Kerry, T. and Tollitt, J. (1990), *Teaching Infants*, Basil Blackwell.

Lemlech, J.L. (1988), *Classroom Management: Methods and Techniques for Elementary and Secondary Teachers*, Longman.

Pascall, C. (1990), *Under Fives in the Infant Classroom*, Trentham Books.

Yeomans, R. (1987), 'Making the Large Group Feel Small', *Cambridge Journal of Education* **17(3)**.

7
■ ■ ■

Managing Classroom Resources to Support Learning

JOHN KEYS

The successful primary teacher needs to be a successful manager; managing not only the day-to-day needs of pupils, but also managing the planning and process of the National Curriculum, evaluation and assessment, managing time, resources, classroom assistants and other adults.

Successfully managing the learning resources in the modern primary school is crucial to efficient and effective pupil learning. The 'thoughtfully' equipped classroom supports more effectively the processes of teaching and learning. A well-resourced classroom reflects the clarity of purpose that the job of primary teaching today demands. A careful selection process will have taken place to provide resources that meet the needs of the children, the requirements of teaching the National Curriculum and the personal choices of the individual teacher. The diversity of resources that aid the quality of learning, teaching and achievement will be a reflection of the values, attitudes and ethos the teacher wishes to reinforce in her classroom. The degree to which this is achieved will depend upon the enthusiasm, skill and commitment of the teacher. Effective management of resources used by the children and the teacher is at the very centre of teaching and learning.

Most teachers do not begin their teaching with an empty classroom – they arrive in a classroom already cluttered with 'squirrel acquisitions' from many previous occupants of the room – the old and tested reading materials, dog-eared with well-thumbed pages; paint brushes that have seen better days, glue brushes that have already glued fleets of battleships together, paint pots and palettes encrusted with years of power colour and PVA paint, technical aids that have lost parts, batteries run down, crucial parts missing; none of which the prudent, ever resourceful, teacher would dream of consigning to the rubbish bin 'in case they might come in useful'! Years of accumulated outdated maths equipment lie side by side with pocket calculators, computers and sophisticated timers and measuring devices, all taking up valuable space in cupboards and on shelves, probably awaiting the proverbial wheel to come full circle when they will be fashionable and useful once again. It is on the book shelves that the power of 'squirrelling' will be most visible; tired, worn-out classics and favourites held together with tape. Many are the favourites of the teachers, long out of print, but still they appear on the shelves of the pre-millennium primary classrooms. We need to ask why, when there is a treasure of wonderful, beautiful books, many of which are works of art themselves that fully deserve to be available to discerning children? Teachers need to remember that classroom junk, clutter and worn-out equipment will hinder the learning process rather than support it.

The classroom of the twenty-first century will need to be much supported by materials and resources that are sharper and clearer in the way they are organised for learning, for researching and for independent investigation. The key to successful, efficient resourcing will be through individual teachers making choices about what they will include and thus exclude in the classroom. For most teachers this will still seem a wasteful, even heart-rending process. Many of them will have learnt to survive on precious little in terms of resources over the years. The very notion of the 'black-bag attack' on such precious reserves runs against natural hoarding instincts. But teachers should be constantly asking what are the essential, most important resources that all pupils should have readily available to guarantee excellence, motivate pupils and aid them in their teaching.

The choice of what is a classroom resource should be one in which the teacher asks herself 'Is this item about quality and will it support children's learning?' Questions about quality must always be at the forefront of decisions about resources.

What are classroom resources?

If you could start with an empty classroom, what would you want to put into it? Few teachers ever arrive at this golden point in teaching, but it is a good point to start the pondering, strip the room in the mind and decide what shall go into it.

The notion of 'quality' should be the prime consideration for inclusion within the carefully considered classroom environment. Resources that support independent learning should have precedence and should be freely accessible to children. The classroom is the 'workshop' for children and they need to have the right tools to be able to learn independently and collectively. Everything placed in the classroom should support the learning taking place, the values and ethos of the classroom and school.

Such a classroom would be seen by the teacher and the children working in it as a workshop, library, laboratory; full of materials that support the quality of learning, understanding and experience. The room would be lively, exciting and visually attractive. Resources and materials would be appropriate to the learning activity taking place; *the mathematics area*, with evidence of current topics, models to investigate, games to extend thinking, materials that allow exploration of time, space, distance, number and logic; *the literacy area* that opens up further reading in poetry, myth, legend and imagination and provides opportunities to write in a variety of fashions for many different audiences; *the science area*, full of opportunities to discover, explore and search out answers, to follow the journeys of Charles Darwin and see the beauty of the natural world he first discovered, to measure and compare, day by day, scientific phenomena such as temperature, precipitation, humidity. The resources would reflect the current scientific emphasis; a range of weather instruments, models of human anatomy, measuring devices, materials supporting exploration of light, sound, forces, etc.

The same classroom would display quality work by a range of children, demon-strating observational and creative skills using a wide variety of materials – fabrics, paints, inks, pastels – skilfully mounted and presented by children and the teacher. Everything in the classroom would have been carefully considered by the teacher, each item, display, piece of equipment, resource would have been selected for a reason.

If we take for granted, the day-to-day essential items (writing materials, stationery, etc.) the next most essential resource will be the *book provision*. Because teachers not only love books so much, and aim to instil such love in their children, they are also incredibly reluctant to part with anything that smacks of a good read, or is seen as literature. But the wonderful selection of books that is currently available for class and school libraries is so vast and exciting that replacement should be a stimulating and worthwhile experience for them and for their pupils.

Every teacher needs to audit their book provision annually – reading schemes, library corners, books supporting the curriculum – to ensure a measure of quality and value. We have to recognise that all resources, and especially well-used books, have a 'sell by date'; wear out, become tattered and torn and thus lack any quality whatsoever. At this point the professional, quality-conscious teacher is going to consider the 'black-bag attack' approach! This sometimes hurts!

An occasion such as a change of classroom or year group is also a good time to begin the weeding-out process. A good basic rule is to 'be tough', be decisive and ask the basic question 'has this book supported the significant learning of any child in my class in recent months?' If the answer is 'no' then its value is suspect and could confidently be assigned to the black bag. The space created by its absence could now well be used to up-grade the existing book provision with new books that *will* play a more central role in the learning process.

A major resource, seldom considered by experienced teachers and those training the teachers of the next century, is the *teaching focus* of the classroom – the blackboard, and its modern day equivalent, the white board – the chalkface of the classroom!

Whatever its form, the teacher needs a place to inform, direct, set the question, work out an answer, to *teach* a crucial learning point with groups and the whole class. The 'teaching-front' should also be thoughtfully considered in the same way that all other classroom resources are. Indeed, many would say that the blackboard is a key resource and that teachers as a group have lost the use of this powerful teaching tool. Others would reply that other methods of conveying the teaching are used instead: the OHP and flip-chart, work cards, and individual learning systems. There is no denying that the teaching front has made a powerful resurgence, especially with the recent revival of the notion of more whole-class and more direct group teaching.

Depending upon space, the modern teaching front could include the diary of the week: visitors, birthdays, special school events. Another section could detail specific targets or activities to be completed and what most children will be expected to achieve by the end of the day/week. The remaining working space will be used to teach; the place where teachers show how, children demonstrate what they have learnt, their thinking and how they work through a problem. It may be true that during the past twenty years or so the power of the blackboard, and its equivalent, has been undervalued and in many instances consigned to a near non-existence. It is interesting to reflect upon Pacific Rim countries – Japan, Singapore, Korea (countries with whom we now have to compete on a global scale) – the blackboard plays a more central role in teaching, especially in science and mathematics than in the modern British primary school.

In many of these countries, and including many European and North American primary schools, 'teaching-front' resources in most classrooms include a range of world and local maps, charts and plans that can be brought down from rolls suspended above the blackboard.

Teaching-front resources have not been well developed in many of our primary schools in the past twenty years or so but well-organised and creative teachers can improve these underrated resources significantly to influence radically the quality of teaching and learning.

Structuring the resources

It is essential that both school and classroom resources – materials and equipment – are well organised and structured to avoid unnecessary duplication and cost, and that areas of under-resourcing are identified. A critical question should be: do the resources I have available to me have a clear purpose? Many teachers find it useful to analyse their classroom resource needs using headings such as those in Figure 7.1.

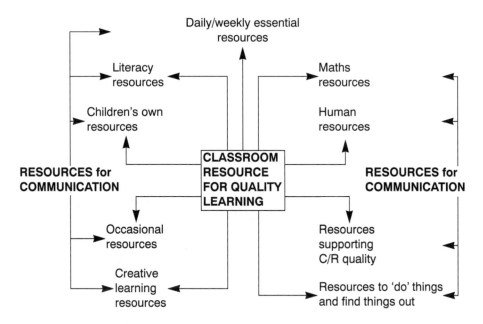

Figure 7.1: Identifying specific learning support resources

Day-to-day resources

Every classroom has a minimum requirement for consumable materials, the tools to do the job, and a successful classroom will be well equipped with such materials and equipment. These items will be in constant use. Many are best kept by children themselves who should be urged to be responsible for them.

Others will be communal but a sense of responsibility towards them is still important, right from the very earliest years. Most teachers show their creative talents when storing them methodically, on desktops or in designated areas within the classroom. Labelled commercial storage units, boxes and trays are ideal for these items, but children also delight in making their own desk-tidies from a range of materials.

The essential point to remember is that these resources need to reflect quality just as much as other equipment and materials in the classroom. Pride in the classroom is demonstrated by the creative and stimulating way these resources are stored.

Literacy and Maths Resources

The well-resourced classroom will have an abundance of good quality literacy and maths equipment and materials freely available. Literacy and mathematics are the cornerstones to accessing successfully other areas of the curriculum and it is right that all teachers pay particular attention to providing rich and encouraging resources that support these important areas of experience.

The writers corner, or literacy area, should be one of the main focus points of a primary classroom; a place to display the best, to provoke thought and action, to generate interest, ignite imagination. Beautiful books, well illustrated, and on a variety of themes can be displayed alongside appropriate real objects. The poem of the week can be displayed here, with postcard-sized copies for children to take home to read and enjoy with their families, or to be used for a handwriting activity, to be put into a homemade bound book, dedicated to poetry.

The area can be used to generate a love of and interest in great literature, Chaucer, Shakespeare and Dickens, alongside modern authors as judged appropriate by the teacher. The literary nature of the area can be emphasised with a range of magazines and newspapers, poetry books, dictionaries and electronic word-search tools. A variety of pens (for lettering, drawing and writing), inks, felt-tips and other writing tools, along with a variety of good quality writing paper, bring a sense of importance to this area of the classroom.

Writing liners (papers with heavy lines drawn on them to place under plain paper to guide writing), laminated for longer use, should be available in different sizes and line spacing so that children can choose appropriately the materials they intend to use in their current work.

The laptop or word processor, conveniently placed within the area emphasises the importance of modern technology in the writing process. All children should feel both comfortable and competent with such technology by the time they reach the upper primary years. By this time children should be making their own decisions about how, and with what materials, they will present their finished pieces of work.

The mathematics area should aim to excite children and encourage a love of the subject. As Galileo said: '*Mathematics is the language in which God wrote the universe*'. Effective management of this important curriculum area will allow children to explore in a creative and stimulating way the world of pattern, number, algebra; to measure, weigh and calculate; to cut and stick; to make models accurately; to carry out investigations; to find out about famous mathematicians and how they have influenced the world through their love of mathematics. A range of suitable and appropriate mathematical tools will be evident within the classroom encouraging enjoyment in mathematics: tools for counting, devices for measuring and weighing, calculators and computers with carefully chosen programs that support the learning at every level. Some supporting the learning at elementary levels and those of greater interest to more able pupils.

If we are to catch up with Pacific Rim countries in terms of mathematical competence there is probably no better way than teachers thoughtfully managing mathematics to make a rich mathematical environment within the classroom that excites and stimulates interest so that children are no longer afraid of mathematics but see it as another world of adventure and knowledge.

Topic resources

In many schools science, history, and geography are taught through interrelated, cross-curricular topics. These also have specific resourcing implications.

Science is an area of the curriculum that has increased in importance since the introduction of the National Curriculum and many expensive commercial packages are available to support each science theme. Many teachers also encourage their children to bring in scrap materials that can also be used in science teaching. Certain scientific items should always be available and children encouraged to use them as young 'scientists': thermometers, balance and scales, magnets, mirrors and lenses, batteries, wires and bulbs, etc.

The same applies to history and geography. Equipment and materials are gathered together for the period of the topic and then put away. Nevertheless, there are items that should be constantly available: a good quality globe and atlas, maps of the locality, photographs of historically interesting places, galleries and museums. A series of key questions can lead children to find out and investigate on their own.

Many items will be required for only a short period of time and 'where to store things' when not in use will be a question that teachers in each school will need to address. Some schools manage such resources by having a room set aside for storage, items carefully boxed, labelled and indexed. Others make use of corridors, corners and other small spaces to provide a living museum of many of these items. Teachers have, over many years, learnt to be inventive and creative in working out where and how to store equipment.

Resources for creative learning

Primary schools in England and Wales are famous throughout the world for the stimulating environment that they create. The primary school classroom that is visually attractive, with displays of children's work both in the class-room and in its public areas is a hallmark of the tradition and importance given to creative education. Examples of children's paintings, print and fabric work can be found in any primary school, and usually displayed in a quality way that is less common in other countries both in other parts of Europe and in the wider world. This reflects the importance British primary teachers place on the value of *all* creative subjects. Resources supporting creative learning activities include materials to paint and draw, print and make books, clay, wood, fabrics, wool, threads and cottons.

Many schools now have a central collection of high-quality prints of famous paintings by world artists. Such a collection can be catalogued and stored in an accessible map chest or suitable large-drawer unit. Each print can be numbered and sub-catalogued according to topic: water, landscapes, people, etc. A booking-out system by children and staff should be encouraged.

Displays of an artistic theme set up in the classroom can direct pupils' attention to specific areas of the prints, for which a small rectangular 'viewfinder' is useful to focus the eye on significant or unusual aspects.

The resources for music are more likely to be centrally held and will normally be the responsibility of the co-ordinator. However, most primary teachers will want to have a small range of resources available within the classroom; some pitched and unpitched percussion instruments, recording equipment so that children can improvise, compose and perform at any time. Again this may well have a 'space' within the everyday programme, or they may be re-introduced to the class at regular intervals.

Occasional resources

Many resources are needed for just a few occasions during the year and although most teachers have their own materials and ideas for, say, Christmas, harvest, Divali, etc., the school too can have a collection that teachers can draw upon for such occasions. These items are best stored in boxes or tidy trays in designated areas throughout the school.

Religious artefacts, costumes and food from other cultures and religions are perhaps only required at specific times of the year and these too can be centrally stored for collective use throughout the school. A decision will have to be taken as to which of these resources should be centrally held, who will be responsible for them and the arrangements for withdrawal for classroom use.

The class teacher will also need to take full cognizance of the multicultural and multiracial nature of her school, and of society in general. Her resources will include books, equipment and materials that reflect this society. Thus clothing, food, music and musical instruments from other countries will also form part of the resource provision. Much of this is available on loan from multicultural centres and from the children themselves; for they too are a resource we can tap!

Resources supporting classroom quality

The late Mia Kellmer Pringle, founder-director of the National Children's Bureau, often spoke of the four 'needs' of children as being:

- the need for love;
- the need for praise and recognition;
- the need for responsibility; and
- the need for stimulating experience.

The latter two 'needs' have certainly been catered for in many of our schools over the past decades. Stimulating and exciting classroom environments have been a strength of British primary schools since the early sixties and many teachers have take time and pride in presenting quality classroom environments for their children, carefully controlling the provision of resources to support effective learning. The children have themselves become involved in taking responsibility for the care of materials and resources and for being responsible for returning things to their proper places.

The modern primary school has become more than just a workshop for children, it is a place where growth in understanding, love and care takes place. The classroom is where living and learning can take place in an environment of safety, tranquillity and beauty. The good classroom reflects the good home – it should be about quality and beauty as much about efficiency and standards. The use of high-quality fabrics in displays and the placing of plants are as important in encouraging an appreciation of aesthetics, as the provision of good quality furniture and fittings.

Objects made by craftsmen, pottery, paintings, wood carvings, freely displayed both in the classroom and other areas of the school, bring a sense of beauty and awe to children. The primary classroom is an ideal place for children to discuss the skills and materials being used and what it is the craftsman has done with the materials to bring about quality and beauty; what is the craftsman's 'added value' to the raw materials he has handled?

The management decision to make such purchases may well be beyond the scope of many smaller schools, but could well be a matter for a consortium of schools to consider and share the resources. Many primary schools have their own individual collections of old objects in a school 'museum'. These 'museums' vary considerably from school to school; the best often being on open-plan shelving, well labelled, and freely available to classteachers and to children, the objects being brought into the classroom for specific purposes, for example to support a story or poem, or historical or geographical themes.

There is also a need to search for resources from non-standard suppliers; for example the high-quality postcard/poster from the British Museum, the exquisite handwritten prayer cards and poems often found in shops selling religious materials, bric-a-brac from car-boot sales and jumble sales. Many of these items turn out to have a fascination for children and form centre pieces for a great deal of work.

Children's own resources

Collections of children's own work, as 'published' books, albums and topics are a constant delight to other children in the class, across classes and age groups. Many are collections of favourite poems, myths and legends, children's own stories, class stories and diaries of visits they have made. Well-presented, large-scale class books, using the photocopier to increase scale of text and illustrated with children's own paintings are among the most read and handled resources in many primary classes. They are treasured and passed on from year group to year group and provide interest and scope for new generations to expand and make their own.

Now that desk-top publishing is available to every school many teachers are now considering their own classroom publishing process.

Mathematical models and games made by the children can also be used as ongoing resources. A collection of 27 cubes arranged as a soma-cube, tangrams and pentominoes made from stiff card or plastic, simple noughts and crosses boards, can all begin as exciting CDT tasks that can later be used as stimulating classroom resources.

Pupil-made science equipment can also become part of the resources that children can examine and use over a number of years: kaleidoscopes, pin-hole cameras, periscopes, bridges.

Resources to 'do things' and find things out

The modern primary school is little unless it is about children 'doing things' – planning, designing, making – allowing children to feel the pride and pleasure of the craftsman, artist, scientist. A well-resourced classroom or work area will have a wide choice of materials and resources: wood, fabrics, cotton and wool, clay, card, magnets, mirrors and lenses, wire, batteries and bulbs. A range of tools will support these resources: tools for cutting, gluing and sticking, binding. Such materials and resources can be shared throughout the school, many will be in use so frequently that they will need to be easily accessible.

The classroom of tomorrow should be full of equipment designed to access information at phenomenal speed and also transmit information. The Internet will become one of the most powerful means of 'finding things out'. Learning through such tools encourages individual pro-active learning and releases time for the teacher to interact with other children needing support. These resources also need to be monitored to ensure that *all* children have an equal opportunity to use IT. Children will need much 'hands-on' experience and their ability to use the equipment can be fostered through cascade learning; pupils teaching pupils and through demonstrations of what they have been learning. Displays within the class of printed text, pictures, graphs and charts produced by them will promote the value of IT work by children and the classteacher. Older pupils could be encouraged to use IT to advertise school events and activities on notice boards around the school. A computer skills record card, completed by each child, again transfers the responsibility for accessing the equipment and programs to the individual child. An example for upper juniors is shown in Figure 7.2.

IT Computer Skills Record Card					
Name:					
Class and Year Group:					
Strand	*POS*	*Possible Software Choices*	*Activity*	*Software Used*	*My rating of activity: Good, OK, not very good*
Communicating Information	*1a–d, 2a–d*	*Caxton* *Collage* *Music Explorer*			
Handling Information	*1a–d 2a–d*	*Starting Grid Informa- tion Workshop*			
Control	*1a–d 3a–d*	*Instruct Logo*			
Modelling	*1a–d 3a–d*	*Local Study Stowaways*			
Monitoring	*1a–d 3a–d*				

Figure 7.2: IT Computer Skills Record Card

Use of a camcorder by children can support cascade learning and the passing on of skills such as book making, lino-printing and the making of a model. Creative use of the video recorder can also aid pupil confidence in the use of English. Video penpal messages from pupils in one school (or country) to another can become an incentive to gather information, organise and finally present a visually powerful personalised documentary.

The classroom OHP should be a key item for children when delivering a presentation to the rest of the class. Children making and using their own OHP slides will help them to develop confidence in speaking to a variety of audiences.

Human resources

In the modern primary classroom the teacher is less likely to be the sole adult working alongside the children. Teachers today will be expected to manage effectively the human resources supporting learning: classroom assistants, parent-helpers, teachers in training, students on work experience. Managing other people is still a new expectation for many teachers and is an additional planning requirement for them. Each adult will be looking to the classteacher for professional leadership and will expect to be organised by her. Handbooks produced by the school to support non-teachers in classrooms will be enormously supportive both to the teachers and other adults. The booklets should provide details of school routines, objectives, levels of achievement, standards of behaviour, the school philosophy/ethos, etc. Timetabling for adults will be a key consideration; who they are to access, the support that is to take place, where they will carry out the work, time allocation. Children will need to be taught that the same work expectations are expected when they are supervised by other adults.

The school may have to consider the 'training' of other adults, especially where they are supporting language, maths or science. With a range of other adults supporting the learning it is possible for the teacher to be innovative in what she can ask them to do. As they gain in confidence and expertise many can undertake responsibility for individual pupils in reading, writing and spelling recovery programmes, investing substantial time with them over a half-term period or longer. Others may feel they are able to offer a particular skill in maths, science or music, all of which will need careful managing by the classteacher.

Children using and evaluating resources

A whole-school policy for using and evaluating resources is essential if resources are to be key tools in supporting learning and taking children on to new experiences. Where appropriate, a member of staff should be given the responsibility for framing a policy that can support all teachers to manage effectively existing resources and identify what additional resources are needed.

The policy should include statements about whole-school issues such as avoiding unnecessary duplication, central/local storage of resources, the possibility of a school 'museum' and open access to such, storage and future financial provision for new resources. In smaller schools, the possibility of shared resources could mean that a wider range of resources become available to children within a consortium of schools.

Children must also learn to manage their classroom and its resources. Careful training and direction by the teacher at the beginning of the year is an important factor in setting levels of expectation and responsibility. Children should quickly be introduced to the class organisation, location of materials, the systems in place to use and return items ready for the next user. All children should be encouraged to consider the classroom as *theirs* – and therefore, to respect it, care for it and take responsibility for it. Most teachers assign responsibility for areas of the classroom to some children and this should widen to include them all; after all there are sufficient corners, areas, materials, equipment and resources to engage every child in taking on responsibility within the classroom. Respect for the classroom and its materials will cascade though to wider respect of school and community resources.

Children are the best agents in evaluating the effectiveness of the classroom. They should be encouraged to be involved in evaluating materials and resources, thus making them more effective agents in their own independent learning. Getting the children to talk about the resources they have used during the week, or asking them to complete a simple questionnaire about the resources in the room also gets them thinking about what is available and whether they have been able to make use of them, and indeed, if they *can* use the resources! Such a questionnaire, once embedded in practice, will encourage greater individual pro-active learning to take place (see Figure 7.3).

The primary teacher can effectively assess the value of resources in her class-room, and thus her own management of these, through her own observations of children at work. She can assess the ways in which she believes that classroom resources are supporting and encouraging pupil development in:

- self-esteem and independence;
- investigation and fact-finding ability;
- careful and considerate use of resources;
- their safety and that of others;
- respect for materials;
- learning beyond the requirements of the National Curriculum;
- giving pleasure and enjoyment to their learning.

Summary

Successful management of learning resources, in carefully structured class-rooms, where quality and excellence are celebrated, leads to successful learning by children. A rich, well-provisioned classroom is a place of pride for children, teachers and parents.

Such a classroom can also reduce stress in teachers and children since the room takes on the mantle of workshop, studio and laboratory. It becomes a place where children can work like a craftsman or artist, write like an author, discover like a scientist, or journey like an explorer and travel into uncharted territory through the use of books, CD-ROM and Internet. They communicate their findings through a variety of ways, manually and electronically, not just

---

A Questionnaire about the things in our classroom

Think about the classroom and all the equipment and materials we have (we call these our resources).

Try to answer these questions as truthfully as you can. What you think matters.

1. Can you list some of the resources you have used this week:

   English   Maths   Science   Topic
   _____

   IT   CDT   Music   Art
   _____

   Other activities.
   _____

2. What resources did you enjoy most, and why?

3. Which resources would you like to use more?

4. Do you think you need help with any equipment in the classroom?

5. What other equipment would you like to see in the class?

6. Do you think other children respect (look after) the classroom equipment?

      Yes   No

   Please tell me why?

7. Is there any equipment that you don't know how to use?

8. Do you have any ideas how we could improve our classroom and its equipment?
   _____

Thank you.   Name..

Figure 7.3: A questionnaire about things in our classroom

within the confines of the classroom, but across the world to other children. The modern primary classroom is fast taking on a global nature and the teacher is no longer the isolated individual working alone with her pupils. She is now a manager of a huge range of resources that open the educational horizons for all the children in her care.

Further reading

Kent LEA (1995), *An Education for Life,* Kent County Council.

Kent LEA (1996), *Enriching Primary Practice,* Kent County Council.

Smart, L. (1996), *Using IT in Primary Schools,* Cassell.

Straker, A. (1989), *Children Using Computers,* Blackwell.

Waterhouse, P. (1983), *Managing the Learning Process,* McGraw-Hill.

Willig, C.J. (1990), *Children's Concepts and the Primary Curriculum,* Paul Chapman.

8

■ ■ ■

Other Adults in the Classroom

MAUREEN HUGHES

It is becoming increasingly customary in primary schools for a range of adults to support the work of teachers in classrooms. It is widely understood that these assisting adults can play an important part in providing pupils with enhanced learning opportunities which can usefully complement those offered by the teacher. HMI (1992) make the point that perhaps the greatest constraint on the effectiveness of other adults working in classrooms is a limited perception on the part of schools, and non-teaching staff themselves, of the extent to which they could provide support. This view is confirmed in a recent study by Hughes and Westgate (1997a) which suggests that the involvement of other adults is less effectively handled than it might be, and attention should focus upon developing complementary roles.

Research in this area has tended to focus on the role of parents in the classroom and the increasing contribution of other adults in classroom settings has been largely neglected. Little empirical work exists on the effectiveness of other adults or on ways in which their contributions may be co-ordinated with that of teachers, let alone developed. There has been little monitoring of the success of the contribution of other adults, or the implications for pupils' learning which may result from the interaction of other adults engaged with pupils in classrooms.

Adults other than teachers working in classrooms range from paid support (for example, nursery nurses, auxiliaries or classroom assistants) to unpaid volunteer support (for example, parents, community workers, secondary pupils on work experience placements, members of the community). The role and contribution of each category of adult is inevitably different and this chapter considers factors underlying this issue and explores the necessary preparation and support of those working in classrooms, in order to ensure that better use is made of assisting adults.

Nursery nurses, auxiliaries and classroom assistants

Adult roles in the classroom are different from each other; why they are different, and the consequences of their differences for classroom involvement are considered in this section.

All adults must be clear about their differing roles and responsibilities if the contribution of each is to be effective. With qualified nursery nurses, auxiliaries and classroom assistants, it is perhaps easier for the teacher to see them as co-partners in the classroom than when working with unpaid volunteers. Nursery nurses in particular are qualified to work alongside the teacher, helping to plan, promote, assess and record children's learning. Yet the relationship between nursery nurses and teachers contains inherent difficulties, for as Nias *et al.* (1989) argue, it is a 'partnership of unequals'. The reason for this lies in the fact that it is the teacher who takes ultimate responsibility for planning and organising the curriculum as well as management of the class, although the nursery nurse will be involved at every stage of the proceedings. It can be a very sensitive relationship and it is important to be clear about the similarities and differences in the jobs undertaken if we are to work as partners in providing for children's learning.

The teacher and nursery nurse are engaged in a powerful professional relationship. If the two professions of nursery nurse and teacher are to be complementary, greater knowledge of each other's training is necessary, as this will lead to a clearer understanding of each other's roles, skills and strengths.

Nursery nurses have two years training and their expertise should be used and valued; they should not be used just to clear up activities or only involved with the physical well-being of the children (although this forms part of their job description); they should also be involved in learning activities. Nursery nurses are highly skilled in their knowledge of the whole child's life and although in their training they pay more attention to health care aspects than does the teacher they also study the child's stages of educational development. The training of teachers focuses more upon educational philosophy and practice as well as on the subject content of what is to be taught. Both approaches to child education are valid and of use in different ways. They are separate but overlapping and need to be integrated so that each participant is aware of her particular distinctive and different contribution to the development and education of the child.

In classrooms, teachers are operating under constraints of time; there is constant pressure on primary teachers to 'get through' the content of an overloaded primary National Curriculum. This often overshadows all other considerations. Teachers also need to control a large number of pupils and to ensure that pupils are participating in the set activities. The teacher has responsibility for guiding pupils' learning but the teacher's 'management' concerns may conflict with the teacher's educational aims.

Nursery nurses, auxiliaries and classroom assistants do not have the same management concerns as teachers; they are not operating under the same constraints and this frees them to adopt a more relaxed style of interaction which provides pupils with the opportunity to acquire skills and concepts at their own learning pace in a small teaching group. Nursery nurses, auxiliaries and classroom assistants can therefore act as valuable providers of help; promoting opportunities for collaborative learning under the guidance of the teacher. They can create a secure setting for the pupils to reflect on what is being learned and to approach new, difficult or threatening ideas in a tolerant context, for nursery nurses, auxiliaries and classroom assistants are perceived to be an accepting, positive audience by the pupils (Hughes and Westgate, 1997b).

All staff need to be clear about their roles, what is expected of them and what their contribution should be. The nursery nurses, auxiliaries and classroom assistants have clearly defined alternative professional roles to those of teachers. They do need, however, to be fully informed about the children's learning experiences, and the curriculum to be covered; this is essential for the professional satisfaction and development of all individuals concerned. Along-side this, all adults need to have the opportunity to talk to colleagues so that they can work consistently together moving children towards similar goals. This means that all staff should share decisions in planning collaboratively and organising and managing the teaching environment.

In summary, the teacher manages the curriculum and overall classroom behaviour as well as having responsibility for co-ordinating the respective contributions of each adult. The nursery nurse reinforces these roles, and also has a physical care role. Unpaid volunteer assistants have a range of supporting roles (according to their skills), and these will be dealt with in the following section.

Unpaid volunteers

The help offered in classrooms is sometimes voluntary and parents and other members of the community can also play a valuable part in school as volunteer helpers. In any community there is a great deal of enthusiasm, talent and expertise to be co-opted and the forward-thinking school will quickly identify those people who are willing to offer their skills in the classroom.

What sort of involvement can schools expect?

The nature of voluntary involvement can vary from helping with an outing, cooking, sewing or gardening to a regular commitment to help in the classroom, which leads to a more productive partnership. Often a line of demarcation is drawn between these non-academic activities and work which the school considers to contribute formally to actual teaching. The most popular areas of participation in primary schools are in aiding roles (running the library and doing jobs, for example, photocopying, backing work cards, etc.) rather than in curricular involvement. Involvement in non-academic activities undoubtedly helps the school and may be a first step towards more active involvement even if it has limited educational value.

Using adults as just another pair of hands may not be as effective as identifying their skills and knowledge and utilising these to best advantage through delegating specific tasks. However it must be acknowledged that all schools may be at different points along the continuum towards productive partnership.

Is it worth the effort: teacher reservations

There can be deeply held sources of resistance among teachers to volunteers helping in classrooms; they include ideological, psychological, political, professional and practical reservations (Docking, 1990).

Resistance which arises from ideological beliefs centres on traditional views about professional boundaries and the debate about who possesses the relevant expertise in educational matters. Alongside this there is a fear that involvement in the curriculum would further weaken an already insecure professional status. It is feared that professional status would be undermined if it was accepted that adults, with no professional training in teaching skills, should assist in the teaching process. It is important to clarify the idea of professionalism.

> *Professionalism lies in the maximum of discretion to make individual judgements over the core activity of the institution.*
>
> *(Docking, 1990)*

Teaching and learning are of course the core activity in the case of schools. The teaching process involves complex professional judgements based on professional training. Volunteer involvement in the curriculum does not usurp the teachers' professional responsibility; rather it should support it. Teachers and volunteers have quite different functions in relation to the children. The teaching staff carry the responsibility for the teaching process but this in no way precludes others in a supportive capacity. There are many ways in which adults can contribute to this process under the guidance of the teacher without undermining teacher professionalism.

In fact, research studies in this area (Atkin and Goode, 1982, Hewison, 1982, Stierer, 1985) found teacher professionalism was not diminished as a result of volunteer involvement in the curriculum, but enhanced. If adults are more involved in schools the professional status of the teacher is heightened. Volunteers are less critical of teachers after involvement, for many criticisms appear to stem from a lack of knowledge concerning the school curriculum. Volunteers respect the authority and autonomy of the teacher in organising the learning and communicating their expertise.

Sources of resistance to volunteers assisting in classrooms can also stem from teachers' psychological feelings of being threatened through having their work exposed to public scrutiny and their beliefs challenged. The benefits to teachers must therefore outweigh these negative feelings.

Some teachers also have reservations about volunteers working in classrooms based on political beliefs; for example, they consider volunteers to be papering over the cracks caused by inadequate funding which leads to a lack of adequate resources and personnel.

Other reservations are based on professional concerns and include the lack of training on the part of teachers in communicating with volunteers and working with them collaboratively. Teachers also express doubts concerning volunteer confidentiality and unprofessional conduct. They worry about volunteers misunderstanding instructions or 'taking over' or 'dictating terms' in the classroom and they have concerns about children misbehaving for other adults. Teachers may also believe that pupil progress would be accelerated if the work in the classroom had been undertaken by teachers instead of other adults.

Teachers can also have reservations based on practical concerns. If adults agree to help on a regular basis the need for reliability needs to be stressed. If the teacher frequently has to make last minute changes to her planned lessons due to the unexplained absence of the volunteer assistant, she will be reluctant to delegate any real responsibility to the volunteer in the future if it is felt that this support cannot be relied upon. Inevitably the voluntary nature of the work means that there is no contractual commitment; however, most volunteers will quickly see the need to be reliable. Volunteer assistants can also sometimes be regarded as of limited value to the teacher, involving the teacher in more preparation and time both to explain work to volunteers and to implement constructive liaison strategies.

These are fundamental reasons why volunteer involvement in the curriculum meets with resistance from teachers. Innovation proves to be more successful if all parties clearly stand to gain by the change. In the case of volunteer involvement it may be that teachers do not always appreciate what they stand to gain. Teachers are busy people with competing claims upon their time and involving volunteers makes even more demands upon their time in the initial stages. Teachers feel that while volunteers may derive personal satisfaction and benefits from curriculum involvement, involvement has limited value to both teachers and pupils. Although there are good reasons to suggest that there are also benefits to be reaped by teachers and children from involvement in the curriculum, teachers may be unconvinced especially if they have not yet directly experienced the benefits for themselves.

Advantages to teachers from volunteers assisting in classrooms

Volunteer involvement in the classroom can be a source of effective support for teachers and the school and can also have the benefit of helping teachers to feel valued.

- The more the community knows about the work of the teachers in their children's school the more positive they are in support of teachers and the more concerned they are to back up the school's goals (Hughes *et al.*, 1994).

- Volunteer contact heightens the status and professionalism of teachers in the adults' eyes and can lead to better relationships with members of the community through their increased interest in education (Hughes *et al.*, 1994).

- Teachers become less fearful of other adults in classrooms and other adults become more supportive of the teachers' professional skills after involvement (Dowling, 1995).

- The involvement of other adults in the classroom breaks down the barriers of 'mystification' which often surround the work that goes on inside schools.

- The assistance of volunteers also frees the teachers' time for other work and the releasing of teachers' valuable time and energy enables them to concentrate upon a lesser number of pupils and the more specialist aspects of teaching. This eases the strain upon the teacher's workload for there are many activities which volunteers can undertake which will spread the workload for teachers.

- It would be understandably hard for volunteers in the classroom to feel able to support (or complement) the teacher *educationally*. Interview data in Hughes and Westgate's (1997b) research suggests that many supporting adults see their role as being more designed to free the teacher for educative purposes than to fulfil such purposes themselves.

Teachers who use other adults in classrooms nearly always continue involving volunteers in the curriculum (Dowling, 1995). Volunteers helping in classrooms (and particularly those involved in the curriculum) can bring about greater co-operation between teachers and the school community with the greater likelihood of increased educational benefits for children.

Advantages to children from volunteers assisting in classrooms

In a survey of non-teaching staff in schools, HMI (1992) observed that teaching assistants played a particularly valuable role in schools in enabling children to have access to a range of curricular activities which would not be possible given the attention of only one teacher. Certainly, other adults helping in classrooms can provide an extra amount of individual attention with all the benefits to children's attainment and progress derived from that attention. The distinctive contributions which volunteers make include the following:

- Teachers are working under particularly severe constraints, for example, an overloaded National Curriculum, and the carrying out of assessments. Other adults in the classroom do not share the same responsibility for controlling or educating pupils and are therefore less constrained in interactions with their pupils. They can support, reinforce and consolidate the concepts which the pupils are acquiring and can match these to individual learning rates. This will impact upon pupils' attainment in a significant way.

- Volunteers working in classrooms also improve liaison between home and school. They are not operating under the same constraints as teachers and can therefore provide opportunities to link the home and school experiences of the pupils which can also serve to consolidate learning.

- Volunteers also provide pupils with valuable opportunities for increased contact with a wider range of adults and opportunities to relate to a wider audience than they would normally encounter. Pupils actually enjoy, and benefit from, working with a wide range of adults in the classroom. Speaking and listening skills are enhanced for pupils have the opportunity to adapt their speech to a widening range of circumstances and demands.

- Volunteers manage much more often to make space for pupils to talk in classrooms and this enhances both their communicative and cognitive development by allowing pupils opportunities to recollect, make connections between one event and another, see patterns and generalisations in events and speculate about possibilities (Hughes and Westgate, 1997a). Volunteers can therefore provide particularly enabling opportunities for pupils.

Encouraging volunteer assistance

It is not only teachers who experience difficulties in working alongside other adults, for it can often be a problem recruiting volunteers to assist in classrooms because some adults may find the school atmosphere off-putting. This may be associated with unhappy memories as a pupil themselves or because of what they perceive the school represents. Although they may feel some anxieties about helping in school, this is often an initial feeling and adults who feel ill at ease at the onset usually relax later.

If volunteers are to commit a lot of time and energy to assisting in classrooms on a regular basis then there has to be a 'pay-off' for these adults personally. Adult assistants initially may not feel confident about working on an equal basis in school and it is not always easy to bring about the necessary commitment and level of confidence for them to volunteer regular help. This places a real responsibility on staff to build relationships based on an understanding of the perceptions of other adults helping in classrooms.

The volunteers may be unsure of how best to help or uncertain of what to do. These feelings may also be accompanied by a belief that education is best left to the professionals and they are afraid of interfering. On top of that, they may be fearful of not always understanding the teacher's instructions. Volunteers will indeed come forward:

- if teachers can convince them that school does not have to be a repetition of their worst memories;
- if fears about their status can be compensated by reassurances of their value in supporting the teacher in the classroom;
- if the teacher can talk straightforwardly about the expectations which she has of the volunteers.

Advantages to volunteer assistants from assisting in classrooms

Assisting in classrooms can bring about personal satisfaction for the adults concerned, as the adult helpers are given the opportunity to acquire new skills and develop existing skills, especially if they are well briefed for their role and supervised by the teacher.

- Assisting teachers in classrooms can lead to enhanced knowledge and skills on the part of volunteers.
- Helping in classrooms also provides volunteers with the opportunity to develop a better understanding of teaching methods and improve their understanding of curriculum content.
- Alongside this, volunteers develop a greater appreciation of the teacher's task and this informed understanding of the role of the teacher can lead to better relations with school staff.
- Volunteer assistants may also increase their social contacts through helping in schools; it provides volunteers with an opportunity to meet other people.
- Adults assisting in schools also report an enhanced level of self-confidence through feeling more competent (Atkin and Goode, 1982). They believe their work to be worthwhile and effective (which it undoubtedly is) and this leads to increased feelings of self-confidence.

Training for partnership in the classroom

One of the most frequently advanced justifications for other adults in class-rooms lies in their role as additional support, additional that is, and comp-lementary to the teacher. We must not, therefore, neglect preparation dimensions. As the teacher is faced with the constraints and management concerns of controlling large numbers of pupils as well as coverage of the national curriculum, other adults could have a particularly valuable role to play in supporting classroom learning. With unpaid volunteers, an apprenticeship or modelling process takes place in which these adults soak up the unexamined habits of experienced teachers and remember echoes from their own experience as pupils. HMI (1992) reported that classroom assistants often have little training and most are dependent on the teacher for guidance in their work. It is an inefficient use of energy and time to leave adult helpers, as at present, simply to base their actions upon their own memories of teaching from the past when they represent such a positive potential for enhancing pupils' learning. They should be give the opportunity to examine different roles and teaching strategies and consider the implications for their own practice. A strong case may be argued, therefore, for providing in-service work and ongoing support from within the school if other adults are to be involved in classrooms for any length of time and their full potential is to be realised.

If volunteers are assisting in classrooms on a regular basis, advice and training will increase their effectiveness in assisting the classroom teacher. This can be in direct contradiction, however, to the teachers' views that the teaching staff carry the responsibility for the teaching and learning in the classroom and that this responsibility cannot be delegated to other adults. As has been shown, however, after involvement in school, volunteers view teachers with greater regard as 'trained professionals', for example, as a diagnoser, planner and assessor of children's learning. Adults who have received some form of training claim to have gained even more insight, knowledge and understanding of the teacher's role (Stierer, 1985). Involvement in training in curriculum matters enlightens adults about the teacher's role and the teacher's status is heightened in the adult's eyes as a result.

Training sessions also increase volunteers' confidence, competence and effectiveness. This training most frequently happens on site. School-based training varies but is arguably valuable being tailor-made for the purpose. Volunteers are very appreciative of the training they receive and there is no evidence of them wishing to encroach upon the teacher's role.

On-site training most often involves talks to volunteers, workshops or directing volunteers towards suitable learning materials based on their expressed needs. In the best practice, the volunteers also receive regular training from the head teacher who explains school policies and practices. These adults need induction and ongoing support and the head teacher and teacher should be monitoring constantly the work of the volunteers in order to get to know their strengths and skills.

The training would need to begin by raising the awareness of teachers themselves of the place and value of other adult helpers in the classroom, as the key figures in co-ordinating the work of the volunteer assistants at classroom level would clearly be the teachers. They would therefore require support in examining perceptions and practices as to the complementary (rather than overlapping) role of adult helpers as well as considering the needs of these same adults. This would then lead to the development of some straightforward guidelines which would be useful to all volunteers helping in classrooms.

The commitment and time given to preparing and supporting volunteer assistants in the classrooms results in enhanced job satisfaction for the adults concerned and improved learning opportunities for the children. This helps to shift thinking from other adults in classrooms being seen as an extra pair of hands to a member (albeit short-term) of the professional team.

How to get the best out of other adults assisting in classrooms

Teachers often find difficulty in working alongside other adults compared to working with children. These difficulties need to be overcome, or at least lessened, if we are to utilise a valuable resource in the classroom. Since it is now common practice for a wide range of adults to support teachers in classrooms, and since they are assumed to have the potential to enhance pupils' learning, the way in which such adults are used in classrooms deserves attention. So too does the way in which adults other than teachers are briefed for their role. What is (and what is not) expected of them may require clarification; so may their different but complementary functions in relation to those of teachers.

Where the commitment of volunteer helpers is regular, the volunteer has an entitlement to be inducted into the work and to see how her role fits into the totality of classroom planning for children's learning. The teacher is the leader of the team and responsible for unpaid volunteers and paid classroom assistants. Their roles are demanding and different and other adults need to be well briefed and supervised by the teacher if they are to be prepared to undertake their respective responsibilities and tasks.

Suggested guidelines for developing effective working relationships

The following list summarises the steps to be taken to get the best from volunteers:

- When working in school, volunteers should be regarded as full members of the team and accorded the courtesies that go with this role.
- Work out clearly the reasons for involving volunteers in the classroom as this will determine the tasks they are allocated.
- Guidance should be given prior to working with children and involvement should be monitored and evaluated; how, by whom and for what purposes should be worked out in advance.
- It is useful if the teacher can find time for adequate discussion with helpers to find out what they have to offer and to help them relax in the school environment.
- The teacher needs to think about the ways in which volunteer helpers can be most educationally productive when they are in the classroom. This needs careful organisation to use the time and talents of adult volunteers to the full. The teacher's planning needs to identify clearly the role of the volunteer assistant.

- An induction for volunteer helpers should include sensitive reference to a code of conduct; this should include the need for reliability as well as practical arrangements. Whether or not there is a written code of conduct, there will be implicit understandings about the need for confidentiality in relation to information concerning pupils' behaviour and work in schools.

- Many schools have a whole school behaviour or discipline policy which includes guidelines on appropriate conduct for both adults and children. These rules are useful in guiding the relationships of volunteers with others.

- Each member's function contributes to the team task; the expertise and contribution of each member of staff should be valued and there should be a sharing of successes and risks.

- The teacher must also ensure that everyone has the opportunity to offer suggestions and ideas and that decisions taken are joint and participative. There is a need for the team to work together towards the same goals. Therefore it is important for everyone to have a voice. The comments and contributions of everyone should be valued and either acted upon or the teacher should explain why it is not feasible to do so.

- Having other adults in the classroom does need careful consideration, planning and preparation. Everyone involved needs to be clear about their responsibilities and to know what learning is intended (what the class is doing and why). The intended learning objectives need to be articulated to, and shared with, other adults working in the classroom if classroom practice is to be consistent and effective.

- In most schools the staff have clearly defined areas of responsibility for the curriculum and this should be communicated to other adults so that helpers know whom to approach for help.

- The teacher needs to plan for maximum continuity and minimum disruption to the daily running of the classroom. All staff and assistants should be kept informed about daily events, meetings, child health problems, etc. The teacher should take the time to explain why situations (unforeseen or at short notice) are occurring.

- Time must be made for training to share ideas and disseminate information. There should be opportunities for all staff and regular volunteers to experience professional development within the school. There may be opportunities for regular helpers to visit other schools.

- Volunteer assistants should receive feedback about their work if they are to get the satisfaction which is necessary to their continued involvement.

Unless the teacher takes full responsibility for co-ordinating the work of the team the pupils are unlikely to reap the full benefit from the shared expertise of all adults. If children are to have the best quality provision for their development and learning we must ensure that we work together in the most constructive way.

Conclusion

Involving other adults in classrooms should not be seen as the fashionable thing to do or undertaken to impress LEA advisers or OFSTED inspectors. It should only be undertaken if there are to be real benefits to children's learning. The involvement of other adults in classrooms can contribute to the standards achieved by children in a school. At all stages in the process teachers must return to the basic question: 'Why am I involving other adults in my classroom?' and if the answer is 'To enhance the quality of children's education', then the above reflections are worthy of consideration. It is the view of the author that other adults do have much to offer in the classroom context, and so the investment outlined in this chapter (for example, recruitment, preparation, co-ordination) are well worth the effort for the impact on children's learning.

References

Atkin, J. and Goode, J. (1982), 'Learning at Home and at School', *Education* **10(1)**.

Docking, J. (1990), *Primary Schools and Parents*, Hodder and Stoughton.

Dowling, M. (1995), *Starting School at Four: a Joint Endeavour*, Paul Chapman Publishing.

Hewison, J. (1982), 'Parental Involvement in the Teaching of Reading', *Remedial Education* **17(4)**.

HMI (1992), *Education Observed: Non-Teaching Staff in Schools*, HMSO.

Hughes, M., Wikeley, F. and Nash, T. (1994), *Parents and their Children's Schools*, Basil Blackwell.

Hughes, M.E. and Westgate, D. (1997a), 'Teachers and Other Adults as Talk-Partners for Pupils in Nursery and Reception Classes', *Education 3-13* **25(1)**.

Hughes, M.E. and Westgate, D. (1997b), 'Supporting Early Years Teaching and Developing Complementary Roles', *Educational Review* **49(1)**.

Nias, J., Southworth, G. and Yeomans, R. (1989), *Staff Relationships in the Primary School*, Cassell.

Stierer, B. (1985), 'Volunteer Help with Reading in Schools', *Greater Manchester Primary Contact* **3(1)**.

9

■ ■ ■

Parents as Partners

TOM BANKS AND PENNY HICKMAN

Educational partnerships between parents and schools are currently presented as one element which might help solve the perennial problem of maximising parental commitment to and involvement in the education of their children. There are major problems inherent in such an approach, however.

First, in the world of commerce, whence the concept comes, partnerships are notoriously fragile and unstable. Second, the contractual process typically involves the school and the parent, thus perpetuating the perception that education is something which adults collude to 'do' to children. A third concern is that it is yet another hedging about of a humane professional relationship with a formal process of regulation, an implicit suggestion that adults are incapable of regulating such a relationship without interposing a quasi-legalistic framework between themselves.

The reality is that most parents are actually quite pleasant people who want to do the best for their children, but are anxious about what their role might be. Always remember that, for each child, these parents pass this way but once and that, for each child, the path is different. As a teacher, you tread the path many times over your professional career. But the anxiety factor among parents is one that must not be underestimated; it is fed daily from a range of sources – the media, politicians and other family members and peer groups. Remember also that many of these parents may not have had the most positive school careers themselves and may experience several conflicting tensions as they work towards defining their roles in the education of their child.

So what do parents want from schools, how might we confirm this, and what might we do about it? In a major survey, Desforges, Holden and Hughes (1994) discovered that:

- around 90 per cent of parents are basically happy with their child's school;
- three-quarters of parents think that teachers are doing a good job;

- nearly a third of parents do not see themselves as 'consumers' of education;
- almost all parents would like to be better informed about what their children are doing;
- few parents would move their children on the basis of published assessment results.

The project found that parents' thinking about 'What makes a good school?' focused clearly on the humane aspects: 'relationships between parents, teachers, and children' were mentioned by 53 per cent of parents; 'the atmosphere of the school' by 44 per cent; 'the staff' by 41 per cent; 'the ethos' by 34 per cent and 'academic results' by only 16 per cent.

As noted above, parents pass this way far less frequently than do teachers; two or three times is the normal number of times that a parent will experience Year 2 or Year 4, whereas teachers often build a career and amass a vast amount of experience in a particular area of the school. The teacher is therefore appropriately regarded as the holder of knowledge and expertise and as such is the appropriate agenda-setter in any dialogue. Most parents, indeed, regard her as such. But parents do need time and space to build appropriate relationships and expectations, and relationships cannot be forged at a start-of-year curriculum evening which might often take the form of a fairly structured presentation. And an end-of-year traditional parents' evening is usually held when children are about to transfer on to the next stage. At the same time, it must never be forgotten that, in the broadest sense, parents are often the main educators of children in many of the most important aspects of life. The skills and knowledge of their own child brought by the parents should contribute to the understanding of that child by the other adults involved in his education.

The combination of teacher's expertise and authority and parental knowledge of their child can be the basis for an effective partnership in the teaching of reading. As this skill is frequently seen as the measure of early academic success about which parents are quite naturally concerned, parent and teacher working together can lead to support for the teacher and information for the parent. A productive partnership needs effective communication between teacher and parent, a shared understanding of the reading process, and a clear school policy about the role of parents in the curriculum. Prior to working together, communication between teacher and parent should be initiated before the child starts school and thereafter be frequent, informative and seen by all to benefit the child's learning.

Additionally, it is suggested that a predominantly curriculum-based partnership, such as that concerned with reading should not be of a 'contractual' nature, but a personal commitment based on a shared belief about what is in the child's best interests. Belief is more likely to gain commitment than 'contractual' pressure.

What might a reading partnership look like in practice?

Initially, a pre-school visit to school for parents and child during which the parent spends time with the prospective teacher of their child, and the child visits the reception class. The teacher explains the school's reading policy, its operation in the classroom and the desirable commitment from home, as successful teaching of reading greatly benefits from frequent and regular reading at home. Also, while she possesses specialist expertise, the teacher needs to know the child's personal circumstances to inform individual reading programmes.

At this initial meeting parents can discuss and clarify their understanding of the school's reading policy thereby building trust and understanding which is necessary for productive and appropriate relationships between school, teachers and parents. It is important to note that it is a better time to discuss and question the merits of a system than when the child has started school and needs to perceive parents and teachers sharing a common goal and approach. Also during this visit the parents may spend some time in the classroom with their child, becoming familiar with the procedures and demands of the classroom.

What happens when the child starts school?

He is given a book to read and a reading record booklet, both kept in a 'book bag'. The record booklet is used to communicate between home and school, commenting on reading and personal achievements which are shared with the child. It informs the teacher about personal information about work with the teacher. The child experiences a common focus and purpose where all parties are equally valued and respected.

What is the daily reading routine?

The teacher selects appropriate reading for the child and teaches reading in school. The reading booklet is used to keep a dated record of all relevant information. The teacher makes a note of the books being read and comments about reading performance and attitude, and directs that evening's reading at home. She might note, for example:

> 'Jimmy was keen to read today. He concentrated well and read with confidence and enjoyment. He has learned the sound "CH". Can he find the words in his book starting with "CH"? Can he think of any of his own? He didn't confuse "was/saw" – well done! Can you let me know how he does this evening, please?'

The book bag is taken home at the end of school. At home, the parent reads the comments in the reading booklet and notes any relevant information. For example, the parent's response could have been as follows:

'Jimmy found all the "CH" words. He could only think of "chutney" himself. He didn't confuse "saw/was" and is so pleased with his progress. So am I!'

Although somewhat idealistic, these comments are quite typical. The next morning the child returns the book bag and its contents to school. The teacher takes note of any comments, taking into account this additional information when progressing with the day's reading.

This example clearly shows how the reading booklet is used to communicate between home and school, detailing reading and personal achievements that can be shared with the child. The teacher and parent have different but complementary roles which are of equal importance.

A natural concern is that the reading record booklet will be mislaid and all valuable information lost. In reality, this rarely happens because of the value all parties put on the process. Also, the child starts to take responsibility for the process and often he is the one who remembers the book bag, asks to read at school and reminds his parent to read in the evening. If record booklets are repeatedly mislaid or lost, a duplicate record is kept at school. Although straightforward, this is time consuming and realistically can only be done for the occasional child/family.

As the child becomes an increasingly independent reader, and may read less frequently to an adult and more frequently to himself, the partnership continues. Comments in the booklet review reading performance over a period of time rather than each day. Also, at this stage, the child increasingly contributes to the record of his reading, noting books read and offering a personal evaluation of his reading and of the book, and also identifying a next step for improvement. In this way the parent/teacher partnership retains its value for the child, supporting the reading habit and the need for constructive evaluation of performance and what to do next.

Further parent/teacher liaison

Parental involvement does not merely contribute to the educational experience, but is essential if lifelong learning is to be achievable. It is to those closest to us that we look first for approval and from whom we derive the esteem which is of the greatest value.

In *Promoting Quality Learning for Four Year Old Children in Devon* (Devon LEA, 1996), the Devon Partnership Steering Group, representing all those bodies involved in the provision of Under-5s education in Devon, listed the following ways in which parents/carers should be involved in the education of their children:

- through developing relationships with parents and families which are based on mutual trust, respect and understanding;

- through being given the opportunity to accept responsibility for their children's learning;
- through encouraging families to share their knowledge of their children;
- through contributing to a record-keeping system which illustrates their children's progress and development;
- through regular opportunities for social events, group outings and meetings;
- through being genuinely welcomed and respected for their child-rearing practice;
- through avoiding judgements about what is normal or what is best;
- through recognising that each family is unique, and acknowledging and supporting the significance of customs and beliefs;
- through receiving helpful information about the school, its policies and curriculum;
- through valuing and respecting the time that a parent/carer is able to spend in their child's environment, however brief.

Perhaps it would be good for a school to start by identifying and evaluating the planned occasions on which teachers and parents come into contact and where these fit into the overall pattern of the school year.

How this might look in practice

One primary school rearranged the timing of planned parent/teacher contact to try to increase parental participation in their child's learning. The initial aim was to provide a school framework where parents were:

- able to inform the teacher of their child's progress on a regular basis;
- aware of the school procedures and could use them to solve problems;
- fully informed of their child's progress on a regular basis;
- active in the review and forward planning of their child's education.

The following contact was organised:

- *October:*
  An early-in-the-school-year meeting between parent and teacher to talk purposefully about first impressions of school and the child. This was the meeting mostly used by parents to talk about their child's personal circumstances and needs. The school found that a positive contact at this stage created an atmosphere of trust where either party could initiate a meeting at a later date.
- *February:*
  A more detailed parent/teacher meeting when the teacher informs parents of their child's progress and both are fully involved in setting personal and academic targets for the remainder of the school year.

- *July:*

  School reports sent to parents, reviewing progress made throughout the year, commenting on the targets set in February, and indicating ways forward.

  Parents' oral or written responses to the report together with an informal discussion about future aims for the child.

This system of planning parent/teacher meetings is viewed as a basic structure from which further productive contact is planned for each class or year group. For example, Key Stage 1 classes invite parents and children to an informal pre-academic year visit to the existing class to familiarise themselves with the surroundings and classroom management. The school found that this early contact makes the October meeting more productive. Many of the classes in Key Stages 1 and 2 send termly curriculum information to the parents. Also, many classes hold end of topic workshops or exhibitions to which parents are invited.

Indicators of progress

In *Schools Speak for Themselves* (QECUS, 1996), a framework is offered which would help schools analyse their Home-School links. The framework offers five 'indicators':

1 Parents play an active part in their children's learning.
2 Parents are confident that problems will be dealt with and feedback given.
3 The school provides for the social, cultural and linguistic backgrounds of pupils.
4 Parent-teacher meetings are useful and productive.
5 Pupil progress is monitored and shared with parents on a regular basis.

For each of these indicators, both qualitative and quantitative evidence sources are suggested, together with the methods or instruments which might be used to access the information. For instance, on indicator 4 above, the suggestions are:

Quantitative evidence
- Uptake of planned/crisis meetings.
- Parents know purposes and agenda for meetings.
- Time spent with teachers.
- Pupils accompany parents.
- Alternative times for parents to visit.

Qualitative evidence
- Effectiveness of meetings.
- Context of meetings.
- Atmosphere at meetings.
- Agreed outcomes of meetings.
- Parental sense of being welcome.
- Parental satisfaction with outcomes.

Methods/instruments
- Exit surveys.
- Analysis of attendance records by categories.
- Interviews with parents.

It is also suggested that a few in-depth case studies might be useful in enabling a school to learn exactly how communication between home and school actually works. By targeting a small number of specific pupils from different types of background and following through a specific recent communication item – e.g. a newsletter – a picture can be built up of how that item was received and acted upon. Interviews with the parents, either in person or by telephone, can be introduced by ensuring that the person knows clearly that the purpose of the exercise is to improve the school's presentation of information. The resulting anonymous case studies can then form the basis for a discussion of practice and recommendations for improvement.

Another worthwhile exercise is for a small group of teachers, parents and governors to review the school's communication documents for tone, readability, suitability for purpose and presentation. Such an exercise can produce unexpected findings as one school discovered on examining the draft school prospectus at a meeting of staff with a small group of parents and governors. The prospectus was informative, professional but friendly, colourful, well presented and apparently reflected the school which was culturally diverse, creative and believed in equality of opportunity. However, on closer examination, the photographs reflected a somewhat sexist community, with the girls being passive observers while the boys were active and observed. For example, boys were portrayed working on computers and building models, while girls were playing stringed musical instruments. It was agreed that this message did not reflect the school's perceived ethos and a different selection of photographs should be used. More significantly, it raised the question of whether latent sexism did exist and this became a future issue for teachers, parents and governors to address.

After parents' meetings, an exit survey might ask those attending to comment on the time they had to spend waiting, the time they spent with teachers, the attitudes of the teachers, the level of satisfaction expressed with the outcome and any suggested improvements. If parents are invited to complete the form before leaving and 'post' it on their way out, this gives an instant reaction to the experience.

Northumberland County Council's 1991 project 'Starting Out – Establishing Effective Partnerships with Parents' was another scheme which highlighted the need for schools to plan to include communications systems which are frequent, relevant and appropriate and which acknowledge and value the key role played by both home and school in a child's development. The practical results of that project are recorded in the publication *Recording Achievement Together* (Northumberland LEA, 1991) which describes the history of the project and the way in which its results now operate in Northumberland's primary schools.

At the time the project started, many schools already had systems to collect information from parents about their children on entry, but much information was collected in the form of tick lists. Although these did highlight positive achievement, they also showed up what the child had *not* achieved. In discussion, parents suggested that such lists can be threatening; that often, parents ticked statements largely because they were on the list, but with little genuine reflection on their child's actual achievements, and that some achievements that parents valued highly did not appear on the pre-prepared lists.

Parents also suggested that any recording system must allow for a genuine negotiation about the purposes of the record and those achievements which would be valued and celebrated between all the parties involved. The parents were therefore first involved in developing appropriate social achievement 'targets' for their children which were translated into 'I can' statements. It is important that the negotiation of these takes place afresh with each new set of parents so that a genuine sense of ownership can be felt. It is also a vital part of the development of knowledge and trust between parent and school.

Turning then to statements about the intellectual development of children, staff involved were concerned that focusing on achievement as measured by the national curriculum should not limit the breadth and balance of the whole curriculum to which young children are entitled, but that it is important to record achievement in those areas. The learning activities in which the children were involved were therefore considered closely and achievements translated once more into 'I can' and 'I like' statements. These, together with the social statements, were then printed onto sticky label stock stationery.

When achievement was observed, the appropriate sticker was transferred onto a titled, but otherwise blank page in the individual child's Record of Achievement Folder; a ring binder with plastic pockets which had been collated by parents, teachers and helpers working together. In this way, only positive achievement was highlighted for the child, but the curriculum was shared with parents and the perennial question of 'How can I help my child at home?' was answered in a practical and tangible way.

In addition to social and curriculum stickers, other sheets were included, such as 'Special Times', 'I Like To .....', 'Colours', 'Letters I Know', 'Numbers I Know'. There was an encouragement to add photographs, drawings, pictures and anything else of interest.

All groups who have adopted the scheme have adapted the basic system to meet their own particular needs. Essential to the process, however, has been the careful consideration by all concerned of the purpose and methods of establishing the record and maintaining and sustaining the continuing dialogue between home and school. The schools involved have listed seven important issues which they would draw to the attention of any others considering planning similar work:

1 Trying to set up the system without parents' help is extremely time-consuming and less successful.

2 There will inevitably be some children who at first forget to bring their files back to school. But, the more the files have been used in class time, the more the children have taken responsibility for having their own files in school.

3 Where parents are unable to offer a great deal of support at home, then staff at school needed to help the child with extra contributions.

4 Parents with English as a second language may need extra support initially to be able to contribute to the record by mother tongue. Contributions are a vital link between home and school and the record itself has proved to be a focus of talk between parents and staff.

5 Often, parents have become involved in illustrating the statements so that the stickers are more attractively presented. The writing and illustrating of the statements has become a true partnership activity.

6 The illustrated sticker sheets have worked as prompts for those parents who have reading difficulties themselves.

7 National Curriculum headings are only one way of collecting information about children's intellectual development.

The most commonly used stickers have now been drawn together in a publication by Northumberland Education Authority so that schools can draw upon them as they consider their own particular needs, and work is in hand to spread the process higher up the school into Key Stage 2, but not relying on the use of stickers.

Curriculum partnership involving older children in the primary school tends to be viewed with some suspicion and unease because of the frequently undefined roles and responsibilities of parents and teachers involved in such exercises. Traditionally, parents have 'helped' in the classroom, usually with the youngest children, or maybe even provided extra pairs of hands or eyes during a school visit. However, as illustrated by the previously described reading partnership, effective curriculum partnership is possible if the 'grey' areas of responsibility, authority and accountability are clarified. These should include:

- A clear understanding of the role and responsibilities of parent and teacher. The teacher is responsible for the planning, monitoring and evaluation of work. She is clearly the person with ultimate authority in the classroom.

- The need to treat parents with respect and be receptive to their comments, even if they are not always complimentary.

- Careful selection of parents taking into account the task in hand, individual skills and personalities, but not to be selective as the parents represent the social and cultural diversity of the class as a whole.

- The need to maintain school confidentiality and be aware of legal and insurance requirements.

The question then asked must be 'What advantages does a curriculum partnership offer the children?' It is suggested that the following are the most important:

- Parents have expertise not available in school.

- A chance for child and teacher to share cultural differences from home.

- Children are able to work in small groups where their thoughts and voices are heard.

- Increased adult supervision, under the direction of the teacher, allows greater freedom of movement around the school environment and more active experiential education.

Curriculum partnership operating in practice is illustrated by one primary school with a history of successful parental partnerships. Two classes combined for one afternoon each week for half of one term on a Science and Art workshop run by teachers and parents working together. The purpose of the workshop was to enable children to work in small groups of five or six for practical activities. Each group's work was precisely planned, incorporating national curriculum coverage and the children's individual needs. Each child experienced three areas of work in a fortnightly cycle. Some parents were approached because of their particular area of expertise and others offered their services. It is important to note that parental commitment and reliability were essential for the successful running of the workshop. The workshop took place early in the summer term, making it possible to exploit fully the natural environment. Additionally, it benefited from fruitful and purposeful parent/teacher contact during the previous academic year.

The following outlines of some of the groups' work shows how the teachers prepared, supported, monitored and evaluated each activity in collaboration with the parents, irrespective of those parents' roles and expertise outside school.

2 Science groups used the school grounds to observe and collect flowers which were identified, recorded and displayed in the classroom. One group was led by a class teacher who supported the other group led by a new parent helper. The class teacher planned the activity and shared this with the parent. The parent had no specialist knowledge but was skilled with children. He became increasingly independent with his groups.

2 Science groups led by two parents worked together making and using parachutes. Work was initially planned by the teacher and shared with the parents during an after-school meeting. The meeting was used to clarify the aim and content of the workshop, gather together materials, negotiate workspace and decide how to record pupils' work and achievement. Neither parent had specialist knowledge, but both had successful prior experience of working in this way. They used the meeting to discuss ways of challenging children to produce high quality work.

1 Science group looked at changes which take place during cooking. The parent, who was experienced at working with children, did all the initial preparation which was discussed with the teacher, and also supplied all the materials. A cross-cultural dimension enhanced the activity as he cooked Indian food and told stories associated with the different foods.

1 Art group worked with a classroom assistant, who was also a parent governor, making coiled pots inspired by the natural environment. She was very experienced at working with young children and teaching pottery. All preparations for this group were undertaken jointly by the classroom assistant and the teacher.

1 Art group produced a weaving from natural materials. The parent was a professional basket maker but relatively inexperienced at working with children. All preparation was undertaken by the parent while the teacher directed the operation of the group.

1 Art group worked with a secondary trained art teacher learning about colour mixing using powder paints. While the parent was very skilled at teaching art, he worked closely with the teacher, preparing the level of work and discussing realistic expectations for younger children.

1 Art group painted in the school grounds with a parent who was experienced at working in school under the direction of the teacher. The teacher undertook most of the preparation whilst the parent worked independently with the children.

This particular workshop was running during an OFSTED inspection of the school. The inspectors showed great interest in the organisation and rationale of the workshop and were constantly drawn to the activities. They commented specifically about the high quality of the parents; how they were able to engage each child in a group, the quality of questioning and discussion, and how the able children were successfully engaged.

These examples suggest the range of parent/teacher partnerships and the value they bring to the parent, teacher and, most importantly, the child. Whatever form that partnership takes, it is essential that there is clarity in the purpose of partnership and that the respective roles are clearly understood by all parties. Teachers and parents do not bring the same qualities to such collaborations; their roles are complementary, and should not be seen as threatening to either.

References

Desforges, C., Holden, C. and Hughes, M. (1994), 'Assessment at Key Stage 1: Its Effect on Parent, Teacher and Classroom Practice', *Research Papers in Education* **9(3)**.

Devon Partnership Steering Group (1996), *Promoting Quality Learning for Four Year Old Children in Devon*, Devon LEA.

Northumberland LEA (1993), *Recording Achievement Together,* Northumberland County Council.

QECUS (Quality in Education Centre, University of Strathclyde) (1996), *Schools Speak for Themselves*, National Union of Teachers.

Further reading

Bastiani, J. (ed.) (1987), *Parents & Teachers: Perspectives on Home School Relations*, NFER-Nelson.

10

■ ■ ■

Classroom Self-review

MIKE AYLEN

The unexamined life is not worth living.

(Socrates)

Effective teachers have often reviewed their own practice. The approach has not always been systematic perhaps but has taken place when out walking or sitting in the classroom at the end of the day reflecting upon aspects of the week, term or year. Self-review sometimes involves an internal dialogue, for example considering personal classroom practice during a talk about a particular aspect of education or in discussion with colleagues. Increasingly schools include written observations about successes and development needs as part of the teachers' weekly planning cycles.

Self-review is the hallmark of professionalism. When time is at a premium it can determine priorities. It also helps to clarify ideas. Where there has been an opportunity to think through in some depth the underlying purposes of classroom practice it is easier to be more confident in explanations to professional colleagues, governors or parents. Systematic analysis and greater awareness of different aspects of current classroom activity underpins improvement in the quality of learning and teaching. As Pasquale comments, 'Inquiry is the essence of vitality and renewal'.

Self-accountability can help to build self-esteem by capitalising on and refining success and providing the momentum for further development. Establishing effective procedures for classroom self-review is a helpful preparation for an extended professional role in working with colleagues to analyse and develop their classroom practice.

Most importantly, however, you own the process of classroom self-review. At a time when there is no shortage of demands for teachers to comply with external requirements, whether related to the National Curriculum, inspection, or individual school priorities, self-review helps sustain professional autonomy. Unlike some other review procedures such as 'being observed' it is non-invasive but brings with it the opportunity for self-direction and personal decision-making. You decide the focus of what is to be reviewed, the amount of ground to be covered and the pace at which any change takes place.

Unlike some forms of professional development tailored to broader group needs it starts with your agenda, at the stage you have reached, and is precisely focused on your individual classroom circumstances. Nor does it mean competing for a share of limited training resources or waiting until the right course or advice is available. In short it refreshes the parts that other approaches cannot reach. Self-review complements other accountability procedures such as external inspection and quantitative performance indicators. A possible bonus is that your chosen review focus may also mesh with other initiatives such as appraisal development outcomes, classroom based action research for a professional qualification, or school development needs, but this is not an essential requirement.

What do we mean by classroom self-review?

The following approaches offer a realistic means of ensuring regular analysis and evaluation of classroom achievements and development needs. Classroom self-review provides an opportunity for teachers to develop professional skills and strategies for self-analysis and improvement. It involves progressive gathering of information about those aspects of teaching and learning under review and developing strategies for change and more effective practice. The steps involved often follow a broadly similar sequence.

1 Definition, understanding and analysis of a development need.

2 Target setting and establishing success criteria.

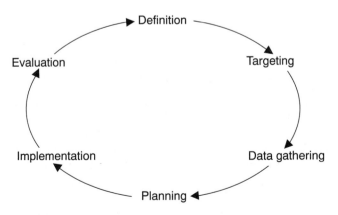

Figure 10.1: The review cycle

3 Data gathering.

4 Planning an improvement strategy.

5 Implementation.

6 Evaluation.

Flexibility to match individual requirements is important and there may be a continuing need to make necessary adjustments and alterations as the review programme proceeds. It is also likely that different issues or circumstances will lead to a greater emphasis on particular stages. As the Roman general Publius Syrus observed, 'It's a bad plan that admits of no modification'.

Practical approaches

So what are the main problems? Basically finding the time and energy, knowing how to set about the task, deciding where to start and knowing whether any resulting changes in practice have led to an improvement. In many ways these are the classic dilemmas of any plan/do/review cycle.

Pressures on time can be eased when the focus of the review activity is narrowed to make it manageable within a limited time frame. Two or three small-scale but effective developments in classroom practice are obviously more likely to have an impact on the quality of learning than a more ambitious project which founders. Establishing a clear time-bounded target at the outset of a review initiative, and listing the possible benefits which are likely to accrue from it, helps to sustain momentum. Although the review cycle provides a methodical approach you may prefer to adapt it to your own priorities and apply any of the guidelines flexibly. For example, the first part of the needs identification stage may not detain you if there is already a clear focus for classroom review in mind.

Above all economy of effort is important. Unless classroom self-review is to be shared with an external audience, for example as part of an accreditation process, rough notes are fine. Reviewing and refining the self-review process over time is useful and widens professional understanding, but the key objective is improving learning through more effective teaching.

The following approach identifies a number of aspects of classroom activity which might be reviewed under the three broad headings of the curriculum and teaching skills, children's learning, and classroom organisation and management. It is important to note the strengths of existing practice. Too often the process of identifying aspects in need of development can lead at best to a formidable list or at worst to a deficit model. The sheer breadth of the current demands upon primary teachers' expertise as 'general practitioners' can be enormous. Identification of the gaps can all too easily lead to a downward spiral, seeing the proverbial glass as half empty rather than at least half full. Classroom self-review is as much about moving from the good to the excellent and developing existing strengths as about eradicating weaknesses.

Stage 1: Definition

Key issues

- What changes might be made to benefit the quality of education for the children?
- What advantages/improvements in personal effectiveness might any new practice bring for me as a teacher?
- How does the proposed review stand against other priorities?
- What are the benefits/disadvantages of the present approach?
- Is the timing right in terms of present workload?
- Who else needs to be involved?

The 'buckled wheel'

There are many starting points for identifying development needs.

One way of tackling an initial overview is to complete the following type of analysis, often referred to as the 'buckled wheel'. The number of spokes and grades can be varied to suit the task in hand and what follows represents only some of the possible starting points.

A mark is placed on each 'spoke' of the appropriate wheel. This represents your assessment of the stage of development of that particular aspect/activity in your classroom. The further the mark is placed from the centre, the more developed the particular activity. Five minutes spent completing each wheel should help to identify and prioritise possible areas for further development. If required a number of these can be combined and prioritised as the basis for a longer term action plan of self-review activities. It may be more satisfying, however, simply to address one issue at a time.

Three 'buckled wheel' charts are shown in Figure 10.2. You may wish to develop your own set of 'wheels' with more or differently labelled spokes as a basis for self-review. Competency profiles for newly qualified teachers often provide worthwhile alternative classifications of key elements of classroom activity. OFSTED's *Guidance on the Inspection of Nursery and Primary Schools* (OFSTED, 1995) includes criteria which might be adapted for some aspects of classroom self-review. Wragg (1993) is particularly helpful on specific aspects such as questioning and explanation. The following list from Johnson and Brooks (1979) also usefully outlines key classroom management tasks as alternative starting points.

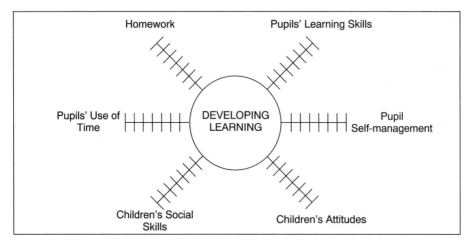

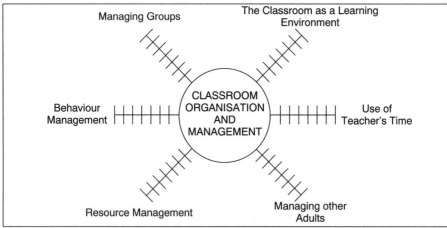

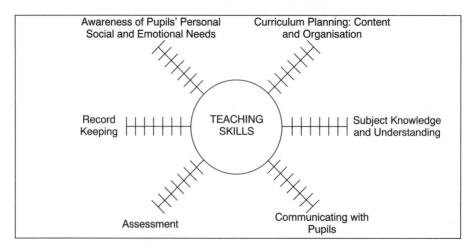

Figure 10.2: 'Buckled wheels'

- Planning.
- Organising.
- Co-ordinating.
- Directing.
- Controlling.
- Communicating.
- Housekeeping.
- Nurturing.

Once a specific aspect of classroom activity has been identified for review a further step is to understand and scope the particular challenges it presents. This may involve a stage of general investigation, possibly through structured discussion with colleagues or those beyond the school with specialist knowledge. Where teachers in other schools are engaged in review activity, conversations and visits often provide good insights into practical issues and solutions to problems. Professional journals, LEA or nationally published materials, especially case studies and video recordings, provide useful information. School policies may provide starting points. A technique often used is to build up a list of key questions about the review aspect in hand. In some cases additional perspectives can be added through dialogue with pupils, other adult helpers in the school, parents or school governors.

Stage 2: Target setting

Key issues

- What are the objectives? (What am I hoping to achieve?)
- How do they fit in with other approaches in my classroom?
- Are they specific and are they clear?
- Are they actionable within my classroom context?
- How are the success criteria to be determined?
- What are they?
- Are they simple to apply and relevant?
- Can they be sharpened by eliminating potentially vague words? (e.g. awareness, understanding).

An early statement of what the review is aiming to achieve is important. Sometimes this is clear and readily managed. More often the intended outcome is hazy, too general or even potentially contentious. The precise goals may need to be redefined or adapted in the light of experience and there may be several objectives for a particular task. Continually asking the question 'How?' can result in action steps and targets becoming clearer.

Nothing succeeds like success. Measuring whether a particular endeavour has been successful, recognising and sharing achievements helps raise personal morale. Success criteria may sometimes be incorporated within the initial target. These may relate to an evaluation of our personal performance or that of other adults within the classroom, improvements for pupils, or a combination of these. Clear success criteria help to achieve objectives more efficiently, expending the minimum amount of necessary energy and making the best use of time.

Two types of questions are useful in setting targets; those relating to the achievement of the objectives and those relating to the process or way in which they are achieved.

Stage 3: Data gathering

Key issues

- What facts, opinions, ideas or prejudices am I aware of linked to the proposed change?
- What specific information is needed about existing practices as a base from which to proceed?
- How can this be most efficiently collected?
- What information is available from different sources about similar attempted change?
- How might it be used to inform this review activity and the choice of information gathering techniques?

Ways of gathering general background information about an aspect of classroom activity to be reviewed were outlined at the definition stage beginning the review cycle. This stage is about identifying information specific to the particular group of pupils and combination of circumstances in your own classroom. It should help to understand a particular problem or development need in greater depth, and to identify alternative courses of action and their possible strengths and weaknesses. A benefit of classroom self-review is that primary teachers are already able to draw upon a unique fund of personal knowledge and understanding about pupils' achievement and day-to-day matters in their own classroom. Used effectively this understanding can narrow the field of information to be gathered, and the choice of classroom data gathering techniques.

In spite of this detailed knowledge, however, standing back from the pressures of the classroom and obtaining an objective overview of the daily pattern of activity can be difficult. By the end of the day, and sometimes even at the end of a session, the detail of what can often be a rich tapestry of events can be elusive. The following strategies for gathering specific information to inform self-review provide useful starting points. Selection of the most appropriate technique or combination of approaches will depend upon the task in hand and time available. Involving another adult in data collection can be effective, for example the deployment of class assistants for structured pupil observation, or of other appropriate adults to carry out pupil interviews.

Care is obviously needed with the reliability of the results and their interpretation. All the techniques and forms of evidence have obvious limitations. Using more than one approach to cross-reference information, where time allows, can be useful as a counterbalance to children's possible concern to please by giving what they consider to be 'right' answers, or to be influenced by their peers.

Where information gathering techniques involve children directly these need to be adapted to suit their stage of development. This can be a worthwhile exercise in its own right, for example where nursery or reception pupils maintain and report upon their own simple diary list of each day's activity, or older infants devise their own more complex codes to catalogue their work throughout the week as part of setting their own targets or analysing their use of time.

Approaches to gathering classroom data can be grouped under the four broad categories of the LOOK classification (McCall, 1996):

- Language based
- Observation based
- Outcome based
- Knowledge based

This analysis is explained in more detail in Figure 10.3.

LANGUAGE BASED APPROACHES

Technique	Possible Applications
Pupil questionnaires/ personal statements	– children's subject/activity preferences – their perceptions of appropriateness of time allowed to complete work – factors which motivate/discourage learning – pupils' self-assessment
Structured discussion with children	– understanding patterns of pupil relationships – insight into children's thinking strategies – pupil's use of/response to questions
Teacher/classroom assistant diary	– use of teacher/class assistant time (e.g. explaining, controlling, questioning, assessing, organising, demonstrating) – balance of attention given to different pupils
Check lists	– monitoring range and purposes of classroom display – analysing suitability and range of resources provision – monitoring aspects of lesson planning – reviewing effectiveness of communications with parents, adult helpers, and other agencies

OBSERVATION BASED APPROACHES

Technique	Possible Applications
Pupil observation	− effectiveness of group work − range and relevance of learning activities used − children's response to specific teaching strategies − match of work to capability − appropriate use of resources − pupils' effectiveness in their use of time − consequences of patterns of social interaction − opportunities to apply specific skills
Adult observation	− impact of behaviour management techniques − analysis of purpose, frequency and type of questions − range and effectiveness of teaching techniques − impact of adult feedback on pupil progress − efficiency in use of time
Classroom video recording	− analysing and sharing and discussing effective practice, and practising observation techniques

OUTCOME BASED APPROACHES

Technique	Possible Applications
Collections of pupil's work	− reviewing relative progress of specific groups (boys/girls, younger/older, recent admissions, ability groups) − comparing progress between subjects − analysis of achievement levels against moderated samples of work
Statistical indicators	− study of standardised and internal/informal test data to diagnose teaching/curriculum strengths, development needs, pupil underachievement − attendance data to analyse patterns and possible causes of pupil absence − reviewing appropriateness of range, relevance and quality of individual pupil data for monitoring effectiveness of provision for individual needs

KNOWLEDGE BASED APPROACHES

Technique	Possible Applications
Information from others	− analysis of pupil's recent records from other classes, or transferred from other schools, to identify achievement strengths or shortfalls − structured discussions with previous teacher

Figure 10.3: The 'Look' data gathering approach

Stage 4: Planning

Key issues

- What are the alternative courses of action to achieve the targets?
- What are their relative strengths and weaknesses?
- How is the overall plan to be represented? (Diagram, list, key headings, stages.)
- Is the sequence of planned activities logical?
- With whom do I need to communicate (if anyone), how, why and in what order? (Professional colleagues, pupils, parents.)
- What records of processes and outcomes need to be kept?
- What resources are needed over what period? (Time, expertise, equipment.)
- What is the cost when assessed against other priorities?
- What is the overall time span?
- What time limits might apply to different stages?

This stage involves reaching the decisions about what is to be done. A simple diagram of action steps to be taken and a proposed timescale are important.

Stage 5: Implementation

Key issues

- What modifications (if any) are necessary to my role and action as the programme proceeds?
- What might go particularly well or wrong?
- What additional commitment or saving of energy might result from changes in practice arising from the review?

This stage begins as the first task is undertaken. It may be necessary to amend some aspects of the objectives or success criteria as this action stage proceeds, possibly to make these either more or less ambitious. While the quality of outcome is often linked to effective planning, luck also has its part to play and positive unanticipated developments can also occur. If problems or minor mistakes arise it's always worth remembering the old adage that those who never made a mistake probably never made anything!

Stage 6: Evaluation

Key issues

- Has the review achieved its targets?
- With the wisdom of hindsight what might have been done more effectively or efficiently?

- How might experience gained from this process benefit future activities?
- Has the process and change highlighted any need for action in other areas?

There are two main purposes for this stage. It is important to decide whether introducing the new practice or development has achieved most or all of the targets and what further amendments or developments would be helpful. It is also as important to learn and gather encouragement from the characteristics of successful aspects as to identify possible causes of failure. Making evaluative notes of the whole classroom self-review process is useful as a reminder when developing approaches to further initiatives.

Some practical examples

The remainder of this chapter is taken up with two practical examples of classroom self review taking place within primary school classrooms.

Example 1 – Developing learning

Stage 1: Definition

Completion of the buckled wheel for 'Developing Learning' indicates a low overall rating for pupils' learning skills. After three weeks with a new Year 6 class, and a high proportion of pupils new to the school, the teacher feels that their social skills are quite good. Children generally co-operate and listen to each other, follow instructions and are able to state their point of view. For the most part they can assume simple responsibilities but lack self-reliance, confidence and imagination in tackling new work. In particular expressive, poetic and descriptive writing is shallow and lacks convincing detail. Pupils' art work, with some notable exceptions, is immature. Their diagrams in science are difficult to follow and recall of detail from a history video programme is weak. In PE, although pupils co-operate in groups, they are ill at ease in commenting constructively upon each other's achievements.

Limited development in pupils' techniques for observation appears to be a common element in these aspects of underachievement. To get a better feel for the general problem, and what might be done, the teacher draws up a list of some of the key intellectual learning skills (Figure 10.4). She thinks through the opportunities planned to develop each of these during the term. Observational skills do not feature strongly.

	Eng	Ma	Sci	Te	IT	Hi	Ge	Ar	Mu	PE	Other
Concentrate											
Memorise											
Raise questions											
Use imagination											
Locate/retrieve information											
Communicate											
(using various methods)											
Interpret information											
Organise											
Analyse											
Observe											
Investigate											
Make/test hypotheses											
Evaluate											
Draw conclusions											
Apply knowledge											

Figure 10.4: Planned key learning skills

Stage 2: Target setting

To improve different aspects of pupils' observational skills in varied contexts, the following targets are identified:

(a) *Observe* and record systematically by use of strategies.

(b) *Copy* the shape and proportions of what they observe.

(c) *Comment* upon features such as colour, texture and tone.

(d) *Remember* and explain sequences of observed movement or other details, and evaluate them.

Success will be judged to have been achieved if after a series of four lessons planned to develop observational techniques in science, geography, art and PE, three-quarters of the class show progress and increased confidence in applying observational techniques.

Stage 3: Data gathering

From lesson activity and work completed so far the teacher has gained a general overview of the levels of pupils' observational skills. This is partly confirmed by looking at some of their earlier levelled portfolio work, although samples of art and evidence of earlier observational learning in science, geography or history are not strongly represented.

Four whole-class activities are therefore planned to provide more accurate baseline evidence of pupils' current attainment levels and to test the hypothesis about weaknesses in their general observational skills.

(a) *Observe.* Pupils observe a model galleon, following work from a recent story and poem about sea mysteries. They are asked to describe what they see and, if possible, to comment systematically, for example working from the base upwards, or from the stern forwards, or clustering observations about a particular aspect. Most find the task very difficult. When asked to devise and write down a series of questions which would help a partner to describe the galleon there is some improvement, however, since some link the process to the principles of a quiz guessing game. Concluding discussion confirms that few children are familiar with more systematic approaches to observation.

(b) *Copy.* Using books from the school library containing illustrations of the work of famous artists, the children are asked to choose a selection of pictures they like. They are required to explain their preference, to comment upon the use of colour and the most striking features of the picture and attempt a copy, choosing one of three media. Overall the results are poor and compare unfavourably with similar work by previous classes.

(c) *Comment.* There is an interesting pattern of roof elevations and varied shapes in a row of houses opposite the school playground. From a vantage point inside the school grounds the pupils are asked to draw these and to comment constructively upon each other's work. The range of achievement is wide, from remarkable likenesses with appropriate proportions and carefully copied shapes, through stereotyped detached houses with little resemblance to what can be seen, to disconnected box shapes.

(d) *Remember.* In a series of PE lessons pupils are developing movement sequences connecting different body shapes. The majority of children are able to describe the key shapes but are less confident in explaining linking movements. They work well individually or in pairs, but are not confident in describing even their own sequence of movements, especially where this extends beyond three elements.

The children's responses to the activities confirm the teacher's earlier concerns and provide a basis for planning improvement strategies.

Stages 4 and 5: Planning/action

Four lessons are planned to improve pupils' use of observational techniques.

Lesson 1: Observing systematically

Science planned for the term already includes work on light sources. (sci. 4.1 a b c, 4.3 a b c, 4.4 c). A class collection is gathering interesting historical dimensions. Following class discussion about systematic approaches to observing items, observation schedules are prepared and used by groups. Each reports upon a different light source including modern and older battery torches, a miners' lamp, oil lamp, signalling lamps, etc. Different observational and recording methods are used including written responses to questions, tick lists, and drawings made from different angles. Groups report back on their work with discussion on the most effective observational approach. The lesson concludes with pupils considering whether the observational techniques they have developed might transfer to other observational tasks.

Lesson 2: Copying shapes and proportions of features observed

An hour after lunch during a mid-October local educational visit is used to introduce pupils to observation frames for field sketching in geography. The work is linked to Ge 10 Environmental change and Ge 1 b,d. It rains but work is completed, observing through the coach window and from a nearby shelter. Most find selecting an appropriate scene to sketch and the principle of observing through a frame difficult, even with help from accompanying adults. About half of the children eventually understand its use in helping to assess relative heights, spacing and proportions of features in their selected landscape.

Lesson 3: Observing colour, texture and tone

The grandparent of a pupil in the class, an amateur artist, has offered his services to help the children. After discussion with the teacher he agrees to set up a simple composition using pottery and glass artefacts for small groups to complete a still life picture using pastels or paints. The teacher is concerned that he appears to have no previous experience of working with children, some of whom are at first reluctant to tackle a demanding task. The results, however, are surprisingly good as the artist explains his techniques, which the children copy, of working initially from the highlights reflected in the pottery and drafting broad shapes. He is uncompromising in requiring them to draw and paint what they actually observe but understanding and supportive of the children's efforts.

Lesson 4: Observing sequences of movement

During informal discussion the school PE co-ordinator talks about some short video recordings of gymnastics sequences he has used with the school gym club. Two examples are used by the class teacher. The children make written notes of the sequences of movement, explaining these to a partner. The discipline of writing as well as watching the recording proves very demanding at the first attempt but with judicious use of the pause button, explanation and careful questioning, some success is achieved at the second.

Stage 6: Evaluation

More opportunities are needed for pupils to practise their observational skills, and to consolidate these by applying them in different contexts. This is not a major problem, however, since some of the planned lessons have the scope for groups to rotate activities and broaden their experience.

The quality of some pupils' imaginative writing improves by applying the principles of the systematic observation techniques learned, to include more realistic and specific detail.

The lesson featuring observation of light sources has enabled pupils to use a wider range of approaches and to record more systematically.

Further practice is needed for the majority of children to use observation frames to their fullest effect.

The quality of the still life pictures demonstrates improved awareness of the use of colour, texture and tone.

Pupils' critical observation of each other's work in PE improves with further practice.

Although the focus of the classroom self-review activity lies initially in the 'Developing Learning' category, in practice it overlaps aspects from 'Teaching Skills' and 'Classroom Organisation and Management'. The teacher decides that this is inevitable for some self-review activities and points up the difficulty of separating interdependent elements.

Not being able to measure the extent of progress in development of pupils' observational skills more precisely is a marginal disappointment. Use of the data gathering matrix raises a series of major questions about curriculum planning:

- What procedures are there within the school to plan and secure pupils' systematic progress in key learning skills?
- Have these been systematically planned and balanced across National Curriculum programmes when they were devised in the first place?
- Is there a need to 'cut the pack another way' and monitor pupils' progress in skill development as well as subject content knowledge more specifically in future?

There is scope to undertake a review of pupils' progress in other skill areas, and to plan appropriate skill development activities during the spring and summer terms if these are required.

Example 2: Resource management

Stage 1: Definition

Completion of the buckled wheel for 'Classroom Organisation and Management' highlights scope for improving classroom resource management in a reception infant class. Space is at a premium, especially when additional adult helpers are present. Key difficulties are:

- an apparently untidy working environment;
- over-dependence upon adults to set out and tidy resources;
- inefficient use of adult time spent upon this;
- children wasting time searching for resources and interrupting the teacher;
- limitations upon pupil independence;
- restricted opportunities for children to learn how to learn by making informed choices about resources;
- occasional lack of care resulting in damage and wastage of resources.

Resolution of the problem appears to fall into three categories:

(a) The quality, appropriateness and range of existing resources to meet learning needs.

(b) Storage of resources and pupils' access to them.

(c) Children's management of resources.

Stage 2: Target setting

(a) The quality and range of resources will be improved in at least one aspect for each area of learning by the end of the current academic year.

(b) The room will be tidier, with resources grouped, clearly labelled and accessible by the end of the current term.

(c) Children will understand the reasons for new arrangements, waste less time and collaborate more effectively in locating and using resources.

Success in achieving the targets will be judged by:

- All children are able to organise themselves to access appropriate resources.
- Pupils are able to tidy away and see this as their responsibility.
- Interruptions of the teacher/other adults are measurably reduced.
- Teacher efficiency is increased.
- Class tidiness, practical day-to-day operation, and visual impression are improved.

Stage 3: Data gathering

To gain a clearer picture of the children's management of themselves and their resources prior to any changes, a matrix (Figure 10.5) is used to record patterns over two quarter-of-an-hour periods. The teacher enlists the help of the classroom assistant. Although essentially a class self-review activity, teachers of other infant classes also express an interest in using the evaluation sheet to analyse the use of resources in their classes.

	2 × 15 min sessions (Note Ch = child) Two children on each table randomly selected (1 = poor, 2 = satisfactory, 3 = good)								
	TABLE		TABLE		TABLE		TABLE		Comments
	Ch1	Ch2	Ch1	Ch2	Ch1	Ch2	Ch1	Ch2	
OBSERVING Can children organise/ resource themselves?									
Are their choices appropriate/knowledgeable?									
Do they tidy away resources appropriately?									
Are they seeing the classroom as their responsibility									
What is their enthusiasm for self-management?									
Response to praise/reward system									
TOTAL									

Figure 10.5: How are children managing themselves and their resources?
(*Source*: Adapted from Kent LEA, 1996)

An inventory of existing classroom resources is also completed against different aspects of learning using a checklist such as that to be found in Kent LEA's (1994) publication *Starting Together* (Figure 10.6).

Essential Equipment for an Early Years Classroom

Large Equipment
Play barrels, large hollow blocks, tunnels, plants, ladders, steps, hidey holes, EDRA or snap boards, balls and hoops, wooden bricks, beanbags, trikes and scooters, water trough, sand trays, large construction sets and accessories.

Small Construction
Sets of wooden blocks, bricks, Lego, Duplo, Mobilo, interlock puzzles, Waffletown and Poly 'M', magnet blocks, threading equipment and graded building towers.

Natural Materials
Water, sand, gravel, soil, sawdust, stones, plants and seed pods.

Small World
Play people, dolls' houses, cars, garages, train sets and bricks.

Imaginative Play
Dressing up items (giving practice in buttons and zips), home equipment, puppets, dolls' pram, shop, clinic, hospital and office play items.

Books
Picture story, information, home-made big books, dual language, community language, story tapes, puppets and story boards, bookshelves.

Writing and Drawing
Paper (lined, unlined, various sizes), envelopes, labels, chalkboards and wipe clean boards, pencils, felt-tips, crayons, chalk, typewriters, clipboards, stamps and computers.

Mathematics
Weighing and measuring equipment, sets of objects, games, building blocks, shapes, materials for sorting, ordering and sequencing.

Science/Environmental
Magnification aids, mirrors, batteries, motors, torches, machinery, tools, plants and gardening equipment, access to animals.

Technology
Computer, calculators, old typewriters, machinery to take apart, moving toys, tools, adhesives, junk material, card, telephones, rubber bands, workbench, wood and woodworking tools.

Cooking
Real cooking utensils, recipes and ingredients from a range of cultures, aprons.

Art and Craft
Paint, a range of brushes, collage, fabric, scissors, junk for modelling, scrap materials, clay, dough, play-doh, plasticine, a range of papers (texture, size, colour, adhesives, sellotape, staples, paperclips, holepunch.

Music and Sound
Bought and home-made instruments, a variety of songs and rhymes, sound making objects, tapes and records (all from a variety of cultures).

Figure 10.6: Essential equipment checklist

Stages 4 and 5: Planning/action

1   An action plan with a time line is drawn up for all the planned actions.

2   Five sessions are planned, including use of stories, to discuss and explain with the children, principles of 'a place for everything, and everything in its place'.

3   A clearer identification of resource requirements in lesson planning.

4   Simple reward strategies are introduced to encourage children and acknowledge their efforts in accessing, selecting, making appropriate use of, and putting away resources.

5   Using results from the classroom resource inventory, additional resource requirements are listed and prioritised. Possible sources are identified, costed and ordered within funds available.

6   Activities and combinations of activity to take place in different areas of the classroom are planned, using the following diagram to stimulate thinking. Possibilities for linked activity are noted and consideration is given to which activities need continuing and which possible phased provision.

7   The arrangement of resources in other classrooms is studied.

8   A classroom diagram is drawn to identify associated resource location and means of storage, having regard to suitable height for the children.

9   Flow lines are drawn representing pupils' movements between activity areas and associated resources.

10 Stages are planned for reorganising, labelling and introducing each aspect of the new resourcing arrangements to the children.

Stage 6: Evaluation

Once resources have been reorganised and pupils are familiar with the new arrangements, the evaluation exercise in the data gathering section is repeated. Results are considerably improved. The teacher also completes a personal evaluation sheet such as the one to be found in Figure 10.7.

There is inevitable frustration that the full range of ideal storage provision is not immediately available but considerable satisfaction is achieved in discarding obsolete materials.

Classroom Organisation/Resourcing Its Effect on Teacher Efficiency and Pupil Self-Management	
	Comments
Teacher interruptions	
Releasing/restricting teaching time	
Teacher efficiency	
Children on task	
Overall feeling of child ownership of classroom/ collaboration	
Order of class, tidiness, visual impression and practical implications	
Organisation and child training similar to/ better than previous classes	

Figure 10.7: Classroom Organisation/Resourcing evaluation sheet

Conclusion

In this chapter I have tried to identify the potential advantages to teachers who use classroom self-review as a tool to improve their day-to-day classroom management. Teachers who have used this, or similar techniques, to evaluate their work have seen many improvements flowing from it. In a job where time is at a premium, classroom self-review is a tool that helps you to make the very best use of all the precious time that you have.

References

Johnson, M. and Brooks, H. (1979), 'Conceptualising Classroom Management' in Duke, D.L. (ed.), *Classroom Management*, NSSE Yearbook **78(2)**, University of Chicago Press.

Kent LEA (1994), *Starting Together*, Kent County Council.

Kent LEA (1996), *Aspects of Classroom Management*, Kent County Council.

McCall, C. (1996), *Supported School Self Review: Rationale and Issues*, Kent County Council.

OFSTED (1995), *Guidance on the Inspection of Nursery and Primary Schools*, HMSO.

Wragg, E.C. (1993), *Primary Teaching Skills*, Routledge.

11

■ ■ ■

Managing a Curriculum Area

MARTIN GARWOOD

Comparing the job descriptions of a primary teacher of twenty years ago with one starting work today would highlight dramatically just how much the job has changed. Nowadays, as well as being responsible for managing a class of children most if not all teachers are managers of one or more curriculum areas, with duties and responsibilities extending beyond their own classroom to encompass all the classes of the school.

What children learn is no longer solely a matter for individual teachers or schools to decide. The publication of the National Curriculum in the late 1980s and early 1990s gave schools a statutory framework for the curriculum. It gave individual teachers a set of challenges: to ensure that all children receive their entitlement to all nine subjects of the National Curriculum and religious education; to become knowledgeable about and confident to teach all these subjects and more, and lastly to play a part in the development of particular subjects throughout the school. These challenges were summarised in 1992 by the then Department of Education and Science:

> *Headteachers must retain general oversight of the curriculum their schools provide and take a lead in decision making about curricular matters but, as with class teachers, headteachers cannot be expected to possess the subject knowledge needed to teach every subject of the National Curriculum nor be expected to keep abreast of all relevant developments. Except where this is not possible in small schools headteachers should delegate responsibilities for subject co-ordination and development to other members of staff.*

> *(DES, 1992).*

Later reports from the Office for Standards in Education (OFSTED) give further emphasis to the need for individual teachers to develop subject expertise and to become curriculum managers. They also underline the value that teachers can add through the successful management of curriculum responsibilities and provide evidence that well-organised and supportive teachers can and do make a difference not just to their own classes but to the quality of education in all the classes of the school. In this chapter I shall look at what this management role consists of and set out some of the practical ways in which a difference can be made. I shall use the term co-ordinator throughout as it is the title which I am most familiar with and encounter most often in my work with schools; a title which hints at the management core of the role but importantly stresses the role of your colleagues working collaboratively with you in what may be new or evolving ways. It is as well to emphasise at this point that the difference you make will be made with and through your colleagues at school, by the application of good practice you are already developing in your own classroom.

Clarifying the task

This subject management role varies from school to school and if you are new to a post your starting point must be to find out what is expected of you. This will reflect both the priorities and stage of development of your school and to a large extent the views and vision of your headteacher. The same Department of Education and Science report (op. cit.) gives a concise view of what government expected:

> Co-ordinators should be given opportunities to lead working groups, produce curriculum guidance, order resources, provide INSET, inform the planning and work of colleagues by working alongside them in class and take part in the monitoring and evaluation of their subjects across the school.

This provides a useful framework to view the different aspects of the role. I shall do so under four main headings; these describe the core components of subject management:

1 Organisation – ensuring that the subject is in place, that there are procedures for assessment and record-keeping, that policies and a scheme of work set out how the subject should be taught throughout the school.

2 Resources – providing and managing resources to enable the subject to be taught; managing a subject budget and planning ahead to update and replace resources.

3 Training – helping staff to develop subject knowledge and skills so that they can teach the subject well; advising upon and providing training to staff.

4 Monitoring and evaluation – checking on progress; finding out about standards reached in the subject and the quality of teaching and learning and using this information to plan future developments.

That's a daunting list of activities and responsibilities, particularly on top of teaching a lively class of primary children full time. The tasks will look less daunting if we look at each heading in turn. Clearly, managing all these aspects will require you to set yourself priorities and to manage your time well.

Finding time to be a good teacher and a good co-ordinator will require careful juggling.

The co-ordinator as organiser

Before the National Curriculum what individual teachers taught was largely the result of their own judgements and planning. Much of what you now teach will still be subject to your individual decisions but significantly more will need to reflect whole school decisions about how the curriculum is organised. As co-ordinator you can play a key part in organising the curriculum and the way that subjects will be taught in all the classes of your school.

A well-organised curriculum that provides for progression and continuity in pupils' learning and coverage of all aspects of the National Curriculum requirements is not completed overnight. It may take many terms but it would be very unusual to find any subject without some level of organisation. After all, most were being addressed before the National Curriculum, and all schools will have taken some action to refine subject organisation since its arrival. What is more likely to be the case is that some subjects, probably core subjects, will be more organised than others. For a new co-ordinator the starting point must be to find out what is already in place.

Co-ordination of a subject will be very difficult without agreement on common approaches. Policies and schemes of work are the basic building blocks of the well-organised curriculum. Let us assume that neither are in place for your subject and look at where to begin. If your subject has both a policy and a scheme of work the following points could be useful in a future review.

Policies come in all shapes and sizes and there are advantages for your school in deciding upon a common format then all policies will have a similar 'feel' for the reader. If you are starting from scratch not all aspects need to be included in the first writing, some can be added later if time is limited. However you go about putting the policy together, it should address all the key elements of how the subject is taught and managed including:

- *Aims* – a general statement of what the subject is for, in the context of the school's own philosophy and uniqueness.
- *Styles of learning and teaching* – the how of the subject; how it is to be planned for and taught; the most effective teacher–pupil and pupil–pupil relationships. This should include a statement as to how much time is to be allocated to the subject.
- *Assessment* – guidance on how the pupils' progress will be assessed and recorded; assessment approaches that are effective; how permanent records will be made and passed from class to class.

- *Differentiation* – what strategies will be used for children with special educational needs and for able pupils.

- *Management* – the role of class teachers and that of the co-ordinator and headteacher in managing the subject and checking on its development through monitoring.

- *Resources* – guidance on the use of resources. This might include the use of community or business links and the place of visits and trips. Guidance should also explain how resources are to be purchased.

- *Health and safety* – notes on particular health and safety issues within the subject area and what teachers should do to minimise any potential risks to pupils.

- *Cross-curricular links* – the potential of the subject to contribute to learning in other curriculum areas.

- *SMSC* – how the subject could make a contribution to the children's social, moral, spiritual and cultural development in the school.

- *Equal opportunities* – how equality of opportunity is addressed within the subject and what teachers should try to do when teaching.

- *Review* – how and when the subject will be reviewed. Putting a sensible date for this will help remind you and all the staff that the policy will need looking at again in the future to see if it still works.

With all these sections to include it looks inevitable that the policy will be the length of a novel, but try to avoid this. Under each heading brief 'bullet points' are all that are needed. A short punchy policy is more likely to be read and remembered than a long one. After all, time is always in short supply. With this in mind, some co-ordinators find it effective to write a draft policy for the staff to discuss and amend. In other situations, particularly where staff have not had much time previously to look at the subject, whole staff policy discussion and writing may be the best approach. As co-ordinator, you need to decide which way of working will be best for your school. Whole staff discussion can be very time consuming unless meetings are well paced and organised.

A policy provides a rationale for and information about approaches to the subject. A *scheme of work* aims to describe what will actually be taught at each stage of schooling; it is a detailed specification for the subject. At best it should provide individual teachers with a map of what to teach and when. Like policies, schemes of work take many forms and need to serve the needs and philosophy of the school. Once complete they are an invaluable guide and will save the staff time in both planning and decision making. However, they do take time to write and this time will need to be carefully planned for.

Schemes of work can be approached in a number of ways. A good starting point is to find out what guidance, if any, exists in publications of your own local education offices and advisory services, as many local education authorities have responded to schools' pleas for help and provided supportive information.

Sometimes this takes the form of complete schemes of work. Adopting a prepared scheme and trying it out for a year is often the best tactic. At the end of its trial you will need to be sure that the scheme suits you and your school and adapt it where necessary. This may save you from 'reinventing the wheel' and will certainly save you time although the sense of ownership will not be as strong and you may still ultimately decide to design your own scheme from scratch. Detail on how to do this would fill this chapter and I shall confine my advice here to general comments. There is useful guidance in the document *Planning the Curriculum at Key Stages 1 and 2* (SCAA, 1995). This provides step by step advice on the creation of a long-term curriculum plan, starting with the division of the subject into 'blocked units' (those bits that are taught in discrete units) and 'continuing units' (those bits that need regular and frequent teaching).

Many schools do indeed design their own schemes of work from scratch and in my experience the most successful ones start with a subject that is more heavily based on those 'blocked units'. Allocating distinct bits of a subject to different year groups and times of the year is an easier process than planning for work that goes on all the time. Subjects like science, history, geography and religious education often fit this bill. With so much that happens frequently and regularly, English can be harder to plan for in this way but all the more necessary to ensure progression and continuity. Starting from what is already covered in each class is a useful way to identify overlaps and any aspects of the programme of study that are missing or relatively neglected. As your scheme will form the central scaffold from which teachers will develop their own short-term plans you must have a clear idea of what to include at the outset. The following aspects of a subject are perhaps the most important ones:

- *Timing* – the term or half-term when the work will be done and a suggestion of how much time should be set aside for the work.
- *Learning Outcomes* – what the children will learn. That is, what knowledge they will gain and what skills they will be better at.
- *National Curriculum links* – what parts of the programme of study in which attainment targets will be covered.
- *Activities* – the most important activities that children will complete and guidance on how these will be differentiated with notes on available resources.
- *Assessment* – notes on how the work will be assessed and what will indicate that the children have learnt what is required.

Just how much detail to include is something for you and your staff to decide. Whatever you do decide it is best to come to agreement, try your scheme for a year, evaluate and then add more detail in the future if necessary. Resist constant tinkering with the scheme, it can be very confusing, and aim instead to achieve a high level of commitment over a short period of time. Later work will depend on the success of your early efforts in getting a result. Reminding your colleagues of the potential benefit to them of time saved later will help to sustain morale through this process of planning. Using some staff development days often works better than several short staff meetings in getting the job done and you will need to liaise closely with your headteacher so that time is built into the meetings programme.

Once complete, a scheme of work will provide you and the other teachers with a plan that ensures coverage, and progression and continuity in your subject. It will make co-ordinating the subject much easier for you to do and you will see, for example, when and in which class or year group different parts of the subject are taught, what resources will be needed and how assessment is progressing.

The co-ordinator and resources

The second key element in the work of the co-ordinator is to make sure that resources are available for the subject to be taught successfully. I hope that you have seen how helpful your scheme of work can be in this by setting out in detail what resources will be needed and when. Your responsibility is also to keep up to date with new resources on the market, looking particularly at areas of the school's work where better resources could have an impact. Resources give you valuable opportunities to provide practical help to your colleagues.

One of the greatest frustrations of teaching in a primary school can be the time wasted looking for lost, misplaced or non-existent resources. You can help everyone by providing a list of the available resources and where they are located. Using a parent helper to track and log resources can save you having to do all the work yourself. Sometimes just tracking resources can be a problem. One school that had this difficulty used a staff development day as a resource amnesty and encouraged all the staff to empty their cupboards. All resources were then set out in the hall, quickly sorted and the opportunity was taken to look at ways in which some of the resources could be better used. In this school the long lost binocular microscope was rediscovered and the science co-ordinator gave staff some useful *ad hoc* training in its use.

Through the promotion of resources and talking to staff about what further items would be helpful, you can provide useful support to colleagues and help to promote your subject. Displays of resources with associated work by pupils put up in the staff room, shared areas of the school or your own room, can encourage other staff to develop their work and gain confidence with using less familiar items of equipment.

An annual audit of resources and discussions with staff to discover needs will ensure that limited funds are spent to best effect. Developing links with local schools, including secondary schools, and with local authority loan services can be a way of acquiring at low or no cost those infrequently needed or

155

expensive items. In small schools, resource sharing through consortium links can be particularly useful. The co-ordinator who knows what resources are available in the school, where they are found and can creatively top up the stock through loans, swops and careful purchasing is already providing a valuable service to colleagues and to their subject.

Although the funds available to the co-ordinator to buy resources for their subject are often small it is still important that they are spent well and can be accounted for. A list of what was spent, at what date and on what items will act as your record and tell you what remains to be spent. The school's computerised financial system will usually do this at the touch of a button and print out a monitoring statement which should then be checked for accuracy and kept as a record.

The co-ordinator and training

Many co-ordinators find themselves managing a subject that they do not feel particularly expert in. In some subjects of the National Curriculum the rate of change has made it difficult for schools to keep up. The first part of your role in training is to look at how your own expertise can be topped up and maintained. Like all staff development this will be a gradual process helped by a careful reflection on your own strengths and needs, within the context of the school's own priorities for the subject. Looking out for courses to attend, reading up on national developments in the subject in the educational press and keeping abreast of books and magazine articles will all help. If funds allow, visits to other schools to see good practice is a very valuable exercise. Your headteacher or school adviser are worth consulting first to help you to locate the good practice you want to see.

It is important that all information about courses relating to your subject come to you. You then get first choice of any that meet your needs as co-ordinator and you will also be able to advise your staff on what is available and build on their expertise too. Having a folder in the staff room or an area of the staffroom noticeboard where course details are displayed are useful strategies but nothing works better than a personal approach to a colleague with details of a course that they might welcome. Whatever approach you adopt, your role in promoting and advising upon training is an important aspect of developing your subject.

There may be times when your leadership of staff meetings and staff training days is the best way of providing training. You will need to be clear about what you will do and plan for a balance of input and activities in the training session itself. Draw up a detailed plan in advance based upon the intended learning outcomes and talk it through with a colleague. Where you can draw upon and highlight existing good practice in the school, do so, this will help staff to approach the training with confidence and see practical examples of what you mean.

This kind of training needs you to feel confident both as a co-ordinator and as a communicator. Working alongside a colleague in a classroom needs these attributes too and is a particularly valuable way of providing training. If circumstances allow, such opportunities should not be passed over as they allow you a glimpse of how both a colleague and the children approach your subject. Two professionals sharing perceptions of a lesson and together drawing out its significant features is a stimulating way to learn, to support colleagues and help to identify next steps. But as in all other aspects of your developing role as a co-ordinator 'think big but start small', choosing to work first with a colleague you can relax with and who will not feel too uncomfortable with having you on board.

The co-ordinator in monitoring and evaluation

One of the biggest difficulties faced by co-ordinators is finding time away from all the pressures of classroom teaching to manage a subject. Nowhere is this more acute than in the area of monitoring and evaluation because it requires you to get a view of a subject beyond your own classroom. It also poses further challenges in moving you towards making evaluative judgements of the status of your subject in school and for many co-ordinators this may be a new way of thinking and working. Before looking at how this can be done it is important to have a clear understanding of why this aspect of the co-ordinator's role is none the less crucial.

A common strand in all of the sections in this chapter whether resources, training or organisation, has been the necessity for you to find out what is already in place before making decisions about needs and next developments. Good planning and development rely on a firm basis of information and this base is built from the kind of activities that are called monitoring and evaluation. Put crudely, monitoring activities are to do with finding out, and evaluation concerns arriving at a summative judgement on the basis of what has been discovered. Although as I have already pointed out all the various elements of the role of co-ordinator involve finding out and evaluating, often informally, what is crucial is that the co-ordinator is gaining a whole-school view of the children's progress and their standards of achievement. That is after all what all these management processes must lead towards – improvements in the children's learning. A school culture where children's progress and achievements lie at the centre is one where the co-ordinator's responsibility to monitor the subject and evaluate strengths and weaknesses is more likely to be accepted by all the staff and worked on collaboratively. So in schools where this aspect of the role is new and may generate apprehension a co-ordinator who says 'I need to monitor and evaluate this subject so that we will all know how best to serve the needs of our pupils', will help to provide a positive rationale. But where to begin?

As you have seen there is no shortage of aspects of your subject to find out about but the most important ones to have a clear view of are those to do with the quality of the children's work, these are:

- the standards the pupils achieve;
- the progress they make over time;
- their coverage of the curriculum.

Your role is to acquire information systematically about the whole school so that you can make increasingly refined judgements. It's rather like completing a picture; a whole school picture of your subject. Over time you must aim to complete different parts of that picture. Some parts may be sketched in quickly while others will be more difficult to complete. The easiest part to complete will be the work of the children in your own classroom and your view of this will provide a firm foundation for the bigger picture.

If we look at standards for example, there are a number of ways in which you already gain information on which to make judgements about your class:

- looking at work in books and on display;
- observing the pupils at work;
- discussing work with them;
- testing and considering the results.

You may also find time to compare work with a class of similarly aged pupils in your own school or a class in a neighbouring school. This helps to ensure that you are not seeing your children's work in isolation and that you are able to make comparisons. If you are doing all these things then you should have a pretty good idea of the standards achieved by your own class.

Filling in other parts of the picture, that is of standards in other classes can be done by using similar approaches. You will need to allocate time to do this but not necessarily time when you should be teaching. If you have some non-contact time it will allow you to actually visit these other classes to see pupils at work and talk about their work with them but the absence of non-contact time does not and should not prevent you from monitoring and evaluation. Using the approaches you are familiar with in your own classroom you can for example:

- ask colleagues to tell you about the standards their pupils reach;
- look at work on display around the school, in shared areas and in classrooms;
- ask colleagues to show you some of the work in their pupils' books;
- review any assessment information available for the subject – standardised tests, SAT scores, etc.

I like to characterise these four approaches as:

- conversations;
- walkabouts;
- documentary;
- data-searching.

All four can be used to help you find out many aspects of your subject. With observation as a fifth approach, they form a useful repertoire of evidence-gathering techniques:

- Conversations can be one to one or to a larger audience. You should not overlook the value of simply asking colleagues their views and setting aside time for this on a regular basis. Staff meetings are a formal kind of conversation and likewise can be used by you to gather information.

- Walkabouts take you out of your room and can be fitted in after school or even in the occasional lunchtime. Their value is that you actually get to see other classrooms, have the chance to talk to colleagues and are seen to be taking a supportive interest in their work. Walkabouts are good for looking at work on display and at the provision and organisation of resources for your subject.

- Documentary approaches take you into pupils' work in books and teachers' planning. All schools differ in their approaches to planning but if half-termly or termly plans are used you should arrange to look at these regularly. They give you a picture of what other classes will do and from this you can find out about curriculum coverage, particularly interesting work to see and resources that will be needed.

An especially valuable activity is to look at pupils' work in their books. It can tell you a lot about standards, about the range of work completed and about the consistency of approach across different classes. Many schools now organise staff meetings when all staff bring a sample of books to look at together. This can be a very valuable activity. If your subject is under review in this way help colleagues to look by identifying a small number of issues. More formalised reviews of this kind can be used as agreement trialing when decisions are made about standards, using the level descriptors in the National Curriculum. It is worthwhile getting your headteacher's support in these approaches and plan to build up staff confidence gradually so that in time you can ask teachers to let you look at a sample of books each term or once or twice a year.

If you can be released from your class during normal lesson time you need to be clear about which classes to visit and what to do there. Most staff are used to being observed by colleagues through the appraisal process but do not take the sensitivities involved for granted. Negotiate your role carefully and consider how best to feedback at the end of the session so that both of you feel positive about the experience. Valuable in their own right and less threatening to staff are discussions held with pupils. Sitting with a small group of children as they talk about their work, respond to your questions and show you what they have done is always informative and will not only demonstrate the ground covered but the pupils' feelings and attitudes too.

However, before you embark on any of these approaches you need to be clear about five things:

1   What you want to find out.
2   How you will find out what you want to know (which evidence-gathering approaches will be most suitable).
3   What time can you make available and how you will use any time released from your class teaching if available.
4   What the implications are for your colleagues' time.
5   What you will do with the information you gain.

You clearly cannot monitor all of your subject all the time so you will need to make choices and adopt a manageable approach. I recommend that you plan monitoring and evaluation, or finding out as I prefer to think of it, in terms of both specific projects completed within a certain timescale and activities that you will do on a week-by-week or term-by-term basis. Sometimes a specific project can span a long period of time but more often it should take place over a relatively short period of more intensive activity. A useful approach is to think perhaps of a specific project per term, running alongside more regular monitoring activities such as looking at teachers' plans and walkabouts. Figure 11.1 shows just such a project, set out as an action plan. It arose from a question in

---

English

The priority for the Spring and Summer terms is for us to check on 'writing' and to evaluate the range of purposes and audiences used in both KS1 and KS2.

Actions

− Carol to draw up writing forms checklist for staff to use

(by end of Feb)

− Staff to evaluate work using checklist   (W/B 4/3/97)

− Carol to look at range of work on display around the school   (W/B 11/3/97)

− Staff to bring samples of all written work from 3 pupils to staff meeting

(13/5/97)

− Carol to report findings back to staff meeting and agree next steps   (3/6/97)

− Carol to compile brief report and recommendations, copy to SMT and GB

(by end of June)

HT to book two staff meetings   (13/5/97 and 3/6/97)
Review progress with Carol   (3/5/97)
Release Carol on afternoon of 20/5/97

Figure 11.1: Project action plan

160

the co-ordinator's mind and concerns raised by a visiting adviser about the range of writing in the school. The project is manageable in its scope and quite clearly focused on one aspect of the subject. Some consideration has also been given to how the information will be fed back to the school.

When staff meeting time is available oral feedback to colleagues is always recommended but you should always write a brief report as a record for staff in the absence of staff meeting time and also to provide information for your headteacher and perhaps the governors. Aim to be supportive in your report, alluding to strengths across the school, avoiding criticism of individual colleagues and aiming to identify a few clearly stated recommendations. To be of real value whatever monitoring and evaluation activities you undertake should lead to prompts for further action. These can have many intended outcomes:

- to raise pupils' standards;
- to improve coverage of the curriculum;
- to build on staff subject expertise and confidence;
- to enhance resourcing;
- to more helpful guidance in the policy or scheme of work;
- to help you, as co-ordinator, to develop your role;
- to build on your colleagues confidence in you.

Remember to be realistic in the actions you propose, consider them carefully in the context of the work already proposed and set up in the school development plan, and the many other priorities facing the school. Remember also to think about the ways in which your work will help your colleagues to develop confidence in you, how it will enhance your colleagues experience of subject management and of successful change and development.

Starting points

Over the course of this chapter you have read about the many aspects of the co-ordinator's role and you have also probably wondered about how to manage this potentially demanding job. Managing your own time and energies is going to need careful planning. Having a development plan for your subject will help you to make decisions about where to focus your attention. Figure 11.2 is an example of what such a plan might look like. This 'personal' plan should fit comfortably with your school's overall development plan, but will be more focused. Under each of the main aspects of your role it prompts you to consider a manageable number of things to do, with consideration of the resource needs (time and money), deadlines and what success will look like after the actions have been taken. Many co-ordinators have found an annual plan like this to be helpful but you must avoid the temptation of setting out more actions than you can actually manage successfully!

SUBJECT DEVELOPMENT PLAN		Subject:	For the year:	
PRIORITY	ACTIONS REQUIRED	TIME, MONEY	COMPLETION DATE	SUCCESS CRITERIA
1. ORGANISATION				
2. RESOURCES				
3. TRAINING				
4. MONITORING & EVALUATION				

Figure 11.2: Subject development plan

Take time to check on your plan regularly and to review it at the end of the year to evaluate its success. A brief written report highlighting strengths and weaknesses in the subject, actions initiated by you and priorities for the year ahead will prompt you to reflect on where you are and also provide valuable feedback to your colleagues if shared with them. This report will also be of value to your headteacher and the governing body in their future management of the school. It will help them to understand the strengths and weaknesses in your subject and what needs to be done next.

With so much going on in school your plan and report will help you to manage your workload and provide you with a valuable record of what you have done. A co-ordinator or subject file containing your reports and records, along with records of budget usage, training undertaken by you and colleagues and any evidence (photos, samples of work) of pupils' work will provide both evidence and a record of the development of your subject.

Finally, although much of the work suggested in the section has taken you out of your classroom, this is a good time to take you back there to consider the ways in which your own room can provide useful starting points for your subject management role. These can act as important starting points for your colleagues too. Your classroom can and should act as an informative shop window on your subject, where ideas, interest and good practice are promoted, through for example:

1 Displays of pupils' work that demonstrate good standards and the approaches you value.

2 Resources that are organised for effective use, stored and presented carefully to the pupils.

3 Stimulating, good quality books linked to object, artefacts or equipment.

4 Planning that reflects the best practice in the school.

5 Evidence of your approaches to assessment and some samples of pupils' work collected as exemplar material.

6 Your own notes on how you monitor and evaluate the pupils' progress in your subject in your classroom.

As your work as a co-ordinator develops what will count above all else is the enthusiasm you bring to your subject and its management and the way in which you present yourself as a learner working alongside your pupils and your colleagues. Managing a class and a subject area are challenging responsibilities. The secret of both is good planning and organisation and a positive outlook. With these attitudes you can and will make a difference to not just your own class but to all the classes in the school.

References

DES (1992), *Curriculum Organisation and Classroom Practice In Primary Schools*, HMSO.

Schools Curriculum and Assessment Authority (1995), *Planning the Curriculum at Key Stages 1 and 2*, SCAA.

Further reading

Harrison, M. (ed.) (1995), *Developing a Leadership Role Within the Key Stage 2 Curriculum*, The Falmer Press.

OFSTED (1994), *Primary Matters*, HMSO.

OFSTED (1996), *Subjects and Standards: Issues for School Development*, HMSO.

Sutton, R. (1994), *School Self Review – A Practical Approach*, Trinity Press.

West, N. (1995), *Middle Management in the Primary School*, David Fulton.

12

■ ■ ■

Stress Factors – Taking Control

COLLEEN MCLAUGHLIN

Stress has become part of common parlance in that it is used to describe a range of feelings. Young people and adults talk of being 'stressed' on a regular basis. This recognises that life has changed and that pressure and stress are more common than they were. However, it also devalues the experience, in that those who are experiencing stress find it harder to accept this as a genuinely difficult experience, for everyone is using the word to describe experiences ranging from temporary dissatisfaction on a 'bad' day to feelings of pressure. It may make it harder to take seriously our own feelings and experiences of stress.

The common use of the word also reflects significant changes in people's working lives today. There have been revolutionary changes in the workplace during the 1980s and 1990s. There has been an 'intensification' of work, whereby those in work are often expected to be more efficient and more productive. Accountability has increased and those who work are exposed to public scrutiny more than they were. Job security has changed and the idea of a job for life has been questioned.

Changes in the work of education

The changes described above have also occurred in education. There have been shifts in the teacher's sense of autonomy. In 1990 the NUT, in a report on a stress survey of teachers, charted some of these changes.

> *The abolition of teachers' negotiating rights and job security; the imposition of a contract setting down a rigid list of duties and hours; and a perceived lack of status in the community as a result of Government policies.*

> *(NUT, 1990)*

Changes in the funding arrangements for schools have altered and increased many teachers' sense of job insecurity. The idea of a job for life is no longer true in teaching. This can increase the sense of pressure and insecurity in work. Public accountability has increased and many aspects of the work of teachers and schools are much more public. Teachers are in general more open to scrutiny through inspection, public debate and other mechanisms of accountability. These mechanisms can be pressurising and will affect teachers who care about their professional performance, for as we shall see later, some of those most at risk from stress are the best teachers. Recent events such as the attempt of two individual students to sue their teachers for inadequate examination results have also added to the sense of accountability. The culture of society is much more one of rights than it was before.

There have also been huge scale changes in the curriculum since 1988. The introduction of and revisions to the National Curriculum have also changed the context in which teachers work. The role and impact of these changes are reflected in the findings of which factors are stressful in teaching, which will be explored in more detail later in this chapter. The increased bureaucracy in teaching is another significant change as is the intensification of work. There are connections between the number of hours worked and stress, as well as evidence to suggest that teachers are working longer hours than they did before (Johnstone, 1993). There are also connections between the hours worked, stress and the nature of the work. These will be explored further later. These changes are important for they help us to recognise that there have been real changes in the working environment and so struggles to deal with and integrate the changes are real – things really have changed. It also helps us to analyse the situation and choose our responses in a more informed fashion. It also suggests that the responses to stress should be on many levels and not just the individual.

These changes have not only brought about changes to the nature of work and our experience of it, they have also made working with stress more complex. If all around you are working hard, experiencing the intensification of work and dealing with the profound changes that have taken place: it can make it more difficult to name and recognise your own experience as stress rather than pressure. There can be a sense of diminishing the importance of what is being experienced. Similarly, it can make it more difficult for others to recognise, appreciate and respond to the stress of others. It is important to note these changes because they signal a need to use different strategies for dealing with a changed context. As will be shown later on, there is a connection between the coping strategies we use and stress. Therefore, acknowledging that the context requires new and different strategies from ones that may have worked previously is important.

What is stress?

It is important to distinguish between stress and pressure. This is reflected in the distinction between *'eustress'* and *'distress'*. *Eustress* is the kind of pressure that is found to be stimulating and motivating. The pressure or the 'adrenaline rush' that can be around performing a demanding task can be pleasurable and can provide a raised sense of performance. Many people seek this out both at work and in leisure activities. Too little pressure can also lead to reduced performance. However when the level of pressure causes us *distress* and is related to feelings of threat, distress and painful disturbance then we are experiencing stress. It is when the pressure becomes too much. Each of us has what many writers on the subject have called a *stress comfort zone* (Figure 12.1)

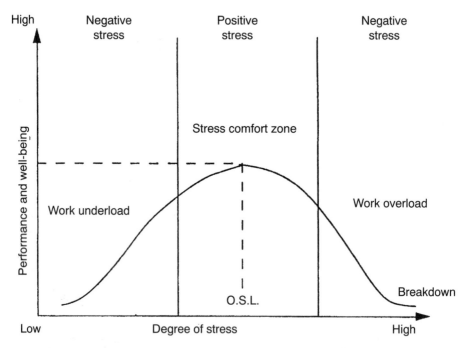

Figure 12.1: The stress and performance OSL curve (OSL = optimum stress level)

So when we are discussing stress we are discussing the unpleasant emotions associated with too much pressure. This is captured in one of the most commonly accepted definitions of stress. Kyriacou and Sutcliffe (1978) defined stress as:

> *a response of negative affect [such as anger or depression] resulting from aspects of the teacher's job and mediated by the perception that the demands made upon the teacher constitute a threat to his [or her] self-esteem or well being and by coping mechanisms activated to reduce the perceived threat.*

There are two elements in this definition worth focusing on in a little more detail. The first is the 'negative effects' or emotions. When we express distress due to stress, there are a range of effects. Physiology, psychology and behaviour can all be altered in the short term. Physiological changes can include raised blood pressure, increased heart beat, dryness of mouth and throat, increased sweating and increased breathing rate. Psychologically we can experience anxiety, frustration, tension, fatigue, irritability, boredom, feelings of threat, feelings of low self-esteem and reduced job satisfaction. Behaviourally we can tend towards more impulsive behaviour, an inability to concentrate, feelings of heightened emotionality such as wanting to cry, hide or run, and we can start indulging more heavily in smoking, alcohol or food. These are all recognisable as actions or feelings that many indulge in some of the time and they can work to reduce short-term pressure, it is the more prolonged existence of these that are recognised as symptoms of stress. In the long term these strategies become unproductive as coping strategies.

Perception, threat and control

The physical and emotional reactions associated with stress are linked to the perception of threat. The reactions are the primitive ones related to fight or flight. These reactions are not only associated with physical threat.

Rather, the perception of threat to one's self-esteem and mental well-being in general is also a potent trigger of this emotional state. Teachers are faced daily with many and various demands: if the teacher perceives that meeting certain demands will be difficult or impossible and that failure to do so will threaten his (or her) mental or physical well-being, then the teacher is very likely to experience stress. It is well worth noting that such demands may be self imposed as well as imposed by others, just as the judgements about meeting those demands successfully may be based on the teacher's own criteria as well as those of others.

(Kyriacou, 1989)

So stress is individual and very much linked to the perceptions of threat. This is not to belittle stress but it is to say that stress is very person specific.

This perception of threat is also related to people's coping strategies. It is when we feel we are not coping that we may feel threatened. Connected to this is the degree of control that people feel they have. There is research to show that the degree of control that teachers feel they have over the demands placed upon them and their ability to control and meet those demands is very important (McIntyre, 1984). This issue of control may help to explain why teachers today appear to feel more stressed than previous generations of teachers. The control they have has changed. Many further points arise from this discussion of perceived threat and control. First, knowing about the cognitive element of perceptions of threat helps us to understand what teachers who are experiencing a period of stress may be going through. It also helps us to understand that our ability to cope changes. What is threatening at one point may not be threatening at another. How we perceive events changes and how we interpret events to ourselves is also key. The events which bring about feelings of stress are real: increased workloads result in an increased sense of pressure. We can intervene on both fronts and this will be looked at later. The connection with coping strategies also signals an area for intervention which will be explored later.

Why should we take teacher stress seriously?

Stress decreases performance and job satisfaction at least, and at most, it causes teachers to leave the teaching profession. It also causes ill health. It also affects the nature of teacher/pupil relationships in the classroom. Recently all the major teaching unions have conducted detailed studies into teacher stress. The UMIST study carried out by Cooper and Travers, with the co-operation of the NAS/UWT in 1990, found that one in five teachers reported experiencing stress. Professor Cooper said in 1990:

> We expected a high degree of job dissatisfaction among teachers, but were unpleasantly surprised by the high levels of poor mental health among teachers in primary, middle and secondary schools ... Against a number of comparable professional groups teachers came out worst on most of the mental health indices.
>
> (Cooper and Travers, 1990)

A similar study undertaken by Cox in 1990 for the NUT found that occupational stress for teachers was much greater than for most other professions. In 1995 more than 150,000 teachers had either taken early retirement or resigned because of ill health; three times the number of those who had left work at the normal retiring age. In Australia stress-related incidents account for 30 per cent of Workcare claims (Rogers, 1996).

This can make for depressing reading. I cite these figures to show that this is a serious matter for the teaching profession and one that needs to be taken seriously by teachers and those who are responsible for running schools; for there is also much evidence to show that the culture, professional support mechanisms and structures of schools, as well as the strategies adopted by teachers can make a real difference. This requires action and serious consideration rather than reaction.

What causes stress amongst teachers?

Even though stress is individualistic we can identify common themes and by exploring what the sources of stress are we can begin to explore the actions to take to reduce and combat it. It is important to acknowledge that objective circumstances do create stress and that it is not just an individual's problem.

If we look at studies of teacher stress we see a consistent pattern up until 1987 and then we see a shift. Studies up until 1987 (summarised in Kyriacou, 1989) identified the following as the key factors in teacher stress:

- Poor motivation in pupils.
- Pupil indiscipline.
- Poor working conditions.
- Time pressures.
- Low status.
- Conflicts with colleagues.

The first two items in this list merit further explanation. Kyriacou (op. cit.) has this to say:

> *Pupils' poor attitudes towards school and their lack of motivation has consistently been identified as a major source of stress in numerous studies. Indeed, it is probably the effort involved in teaching such pupils on a regular basis that forms the single most important source of stress.*

The second item, pupil indiscipline, is a factor that has been found in many countries. Rogers (1996) reports how in Australia this was the most significant stressor for teachers and Esteve (1989) reports similar findings in Spain. *The Elton Report* (DES, 1989) made it clear that it is the consistency of minor disruptions in the classroom that is stressful for teachers. Most teachers cope well most of the time. The top two factors are clearly related to the teacher's classroom tasks and signal an important area for intervention in stress management as they show up consistently in studies of teacher stress before 1987 and after. After 1987 there is a shift in the stressors. The most important stressor becomes change:

> *not only the fact of change, but 'change upon change' Beyond the control of most teachers.*
>
> *(Cox, 1989)*

This has been confirmed in the most recent studies of teacher stress. The UMIST study (Cooper and Travers, 1990) found that the top 10 worries of teachers then were:

- Lack of support from the government.
- The constant changes taking place within the profession.
- The lack of information as to how the changes should be implemented.
- Society's diminishing respect for the profession.
- The move towards a 'national curriculum'.
- A salary out of proportion to workload.

- Dealing with basic behavioural problems.
- Lack of 'non-contact' time with pupils.
- Being a good teacher does not necessarily mean promotion.

The element of being out of control of the changes was significant. This is summed by one teacher in the study:

> Teachers do not object to change as such, but in the past few years the changes imposed on us have got totally out of control.

This signals the need to look at school organisation and how change and development are handled. Clearly 1989 was an intense moment for the teaching profession and one in which these issues were likely to be paramount.

However, the NUT (Cox, 1990) study confirmed these trends. The two most frequently mentioned sources of stress were teaching tasks and classroom situations. Included in teaching tasks were recent developments such as changes in GCSE, the National Curriculum and assessment changes. The third most stressful factor was the organisation and management of schools and the fourth, the position of education in the community. The report concluded, 'Only an organisational approach can help all teachers.' (op. cit.). The report found that the three areas that were crucial to the organisational health of the school were:

- the task environment – i.e. the situation facing teachers as they attempt the job of delivering education to pupils;
- professional and personal development – how well the school develops its staff both as individuals and as teachers;
- problem solving – the extent to which the school staff work together as a team to solve the problems.

(Cox/NUT, 1990)

Cox identified some significant elements of teachers' experience in this and other studies. He reports that teachers feel isolated in the classroom and that the school is a poor problem solving environment (Cox, 1989). He is highlighting some very important issues here. *The Elton Report* (DES, 1989) and other studies (for example Drummond and McLaughlin, 1994) have looked at the connection between admitting problems and competency. For many teachers learning about the classroom and their own practice is a very new idea and there is a fear that admitting that one has problems is to risk admitting incompetence. Cox is a stress researcher and he comments that schools, unlike many other organisations, lack problem solving channels for the central tasks of teaching and learning. There have been many changes in this area of schooling in the last years. There are now mentors, coaches and much more debate about researching our own classrooms and practice. This point will be developed when I explore strategies for stress management.

Who is stressed?

Woods (1989) sees stress as an inevitable part of all teachers' work, since he argues that conflict and particularly role conflict is an essential aspect of teaching:

> *There are conflicts caused by different people's different expectations of the teacher, there are within-role conflicts, and conflicts set up by tensions between the person and the role.*

He saw the following as most at risk:

- Probationary and inexperienced teachers, for they have not yet learned how to cope with the dilemmas and contradictions.
- Teachers who lack knowledge and understanding, perhaps through no fault of their own, of such things as pupil cultures.
- Teachers who found it difficult, for whatever reason, to 'orchestrate' their teaching.
- Senior teachers, such as heads and deputies, who are in the position of greatest role conflict.
- Career-aspiring teachers, especially those in mid-career, who face career blockage, for they lose the main reward that helps balance out the increased pressures, and experience instead profound frustration.
- The caring and highly committed teachers who refuse to compromise their high ideals, and who are faced with increased physical and emotional strain on the one hand and less self-fulfilling performance of the role with less investment of the self on the other.

This delineation is helpful for it reinforces the importance of taking stress seriously. It also debunks the myth and the fear in many teachers' minds that stress is related to lack of motivation. Stress is related to the central tasks of teaching, and supporting and developing these can reduce stress, but you cannot be stressed if you do not care. If we do not take stress seriously we are risking some of the best members of the teaching community. It is necessary also to look at the specific needs and pressures on teachers in various roles and stages of their teaching career. Stress is different at different times and for people in different positions. The research on stress that has been explored so far alerts us to the notion that stress is part of teaching and is related to the professional tasks and context.

Models of stress and the implications for action

In the early stages of work on stress in this country there tended to be an appropriation of largely psychotherapeutic approaches to stress and an application of these to the world of teaching. This model of stress has an individualistic view of stress as its basis. The teacher is stressed because, as an individual, she is not using the correct stress management techniques. In school training days there were often demonstrations of relaxation techniques and questionnaires administered so that teachers could establish whether they were stressed or not. While these methods have merit and can be used to a limited extent, this way of viewing stress in schools is severely limited and has serious consequences. It can place the responsibility for stress at the individual's door and can view stress as an internal problem. This is where some of the anxiety about being inadequate or not being able to 'cut the cake' can come from. David Smail (1996) makes this point very forcefully:

> *Even the currently popular notion of 'stress', which would on the face of it seem to suggest a force bearing down on the individual from the outside, ends up being represented by most therapeutic approaches as something inside people which they have to learn to deal with or 'manage'. Programmes of 'stress management' are in this way directed at manipulating the internal processes through which people are supposedly able to handle stress, rather than at diminishing the stressors in the outside world which have come to make a misery of the lives of so many of us.*

While it is true that individuals can take steps to reduce stress, and some of these will be explored later, it is not true that stress in teaching is an individual problem. Stress arises from events in schools and is related to the context of the teacher's work.

The model of stress adopted will dictate the approaches to working with stress. We need to look at the professional context and not over-personalise the work. As Cox (1990) concluded we need to look at the following:

- the task environment – i.e. the situation facing teachers as they attempt the job of delivering education to pupils;
- professional and personal development – how well the school develops its staff both as individuals and as teachers;
- problem solving – the extent to which the school staff work together as a team to solve the problems.

Taking control – approaches to avoiding and alleviating stress?

Cox (1989) is helpful when he identifies three objectives of stress management programmes:

- to prevent the occurrence of stressful situations at work, or to reduce the frequency with which they occur;
- to increase awareness of such problems, so that they can be more easily and rapidly picked up, and to improve the problem-solving strategies used;

- to treat or rehabilitate individuals [and organisations] which have experienced stress.

Awareness raising

The conditions of teachers have changed and the pressures on the education system are plain for most to see. There is a need to tackle this on a political level in that there needs to be a continued effort to improve the conditions of teachers and to allow for the appropriate resources and conditions for teachers to work effectively. This needs to be part of the tranche of measures used to deal with stress in teaching. This also needs to be acknowledged at a school level. There is a need to raise the awareness of teachers and particularly department and school managers of the issues around stress in education. However, that is not the main focus of this section. I shall focus on the other two areas: tackling the stressful situations in schools and helping individuals.

Stress and support

I would argue that, given what has already been said, it would be helpful to shift the focus to a more positive one that looks at the rights of the teacher to support for the essential aspects of their work. This would shift us from a reactive to an active approach, thus avoiding the dangers of treating stress as an exceptional, individual event. This needs to be combined with a problem solving approach or a reflective approach whereby we gain evidence about the reality of the stressors for teachers in their particular contexts and roles. Research and thinking which I have explored so far (Lodge, McLaughlin and Best, 1992) suggests that there are three areas of teacher support:

- Support for the teacher as teacher.
- Support for the teacher as colleague.
- Support for the teacher as person.

Support for the teacher as teacher

The surveys cited earlier show that this arena is the crucial one and that the two main stressors are related to teaching tasks and the classroom situations (i.e. motivation, assessment). The main focus of working with stress needs to be on supporting and developing the teacher's work in the classroom. Research suggests that we need to target the following areas. First we need to provide ongoing as well as short-term support and development for classroom management, especially group management. The context of classroom relationships has changed and there has been success in working with these areas in schools. (Rogers, 1996) This is best combined with problem solving. Cox (1990) highlighted the lack of problem-solving channels in schools as well as the sense of isolation that many teachers had. There are many methods of peer support being developed in schools today. Schemes such as mentoring and peer observation help teachers to obtain data and to reflect on the workings of their classrooms with the aid of a colleague. These two elements – peer support and a focus on the classroom – are at the heart of approaches to stress.

Another area of teacher support that is important is that of clarity and appropriateness of expectations about jobs and roles. Many teachers are experiencing stress because the expectations are unrealistic. As stated earlier, committed and conscientious teachers are at risk because they will try to achieve high standards. If job descriptions are catch-all, wish lists rather than realistic and appropriate statements of the achievable, then stress is more likely. There are still likely to be role conflicts and issues of prioritisation in a time of such high demands on teachers, so opportunities to discuss and review are also important here. Teaching is one of the few occupations where there is little individual support or supervision of the kind there is in other professions such as social work or in many business organisations. Appraisal is an opportunity for this but it is very infrequent and it needs to move beyond ritual performance to fulfil the characteristics I am describing.

The third major area identified as a stressor for teachers today is change and change upon change in particular. This too is unlikely to alter. What can be done here is to examine institutional and individual responses to change and to examine how it is being managed. The view from the classroom up, rather than from the top down, needs to predominate. Head teachers and others responsible for managing these changes need to try to collect evidence from others on the cumulative effect in the classroom and in the teacher's daily life. This requires dialogue and feedback as well as a desire to collect information on the effects of management strategies.

These approaches are centred on an organisational approach which entitles and requires all teachers to examine and develop their classroom practice in a supportive and constructive climate. It would require a shift in some schools to the organisational approaches to the teacher's central tasks. Cox (1990) concluded his discussion of teacher stress with this; 'Only an organisational approach has a chance of helping all teachers'. We need to shift to viewing stress as something that needs to be dealt with in a supportive fashion for all teachers, rather than a reaction to individual instances.

Support for the teacher as colleague

The organisational and management issues referred to in the previous section are central here. Teachers largely work alone, however, they also need to feel that they belong, are valued and can work together outside of as well as within the classroom. This tradition of working alone has generated a climate in which sharing and learning can be difficult. Moving from a climate of competence to a climate of learning and experimentation is not an easy task but it is one that is very pertinent to stress. Given that change is likely to be a permanent feature of schools and that we are moving towards a 'learning society', we need to develop practices in schools where teachers operate more as learners. If we can shift our perspective so that problems are seen as opportunities to work together rather than as individual opportunities for failure or success then there is likely to be less pressure in a world of constant change and challenge. This requires joint working and more team problem solving as colleagues.

Support for the teacher as person

We are all persons in other contexts and are members of groups, families, partnerships and friendships. This needs to be acknowledged by us in our work contexts, for stress is often an accumulation of pressure in various domains. It is in this domain of support that we can also give individual support when someone is undergoing a period of stress. It is also where we need to take responsibility for being personally effective and reviewing the strategies we use to handle the inevitable pressures of teaching.

There are many things we can do to explore our strategies for coping with work demands. Dunham's work (1989) has shown how effective it can be for teachers to share their coping strategies and that we can learn a lot from those that handle pressure well. The areas we can usefully explore here are: how we manage time; how the classroom is managed and prepared for; how we work with others; and how we develop ourselves as persons as well as professionals. Time management is an important area given that nowadays there is always more work than time. Important questions to ask and discuss together are what strategies we use to manage time; what our most identifiable difficulties are; what goals we set and how we prioritise our tasks. It is important to monitor the hours worked. Johnstone's (1993) work has shown that there is a relationship between the number of hours worked and stress.

All teachers tended to work long hours but those that worked the longest reported the most stress. There is a paradox in that working long hours seems to be the solution but it reduces personal effectiveness after a certain point. Each of us differs in the number of hours we can and wish to work, but each of us has a personal limit. When one is stressed it is often difficult to recognise that this point has been reached.

Others have responsibilities to stressed persons. There may be a need to help them recognise the situation as well as to temporarily reduce demands. There will also be a need to co-ordinate a specific programme of support and rebuilding when a colleague is identified as suffering from stress. The actions taken will need to look hard at the demands placed upon the person as well the strategies used for dealing with pressures differently in the future.

175

Collective awareness of and responsibility for stress and support in a school is likely to reduce the unfortunate and unhelpful tendency to relegate stress to a matter of individual responsibility. Recently a teacher I know suffered from stress. Her school responded positively by acknowledging that the job description and the expectations were unrealistic. Steps were taken to change the workload and to explore other elements, for this teacher was too available to others. She was being too helpful and measures needed to be taken to protect her. The response was helpful as the institutional issues, the collegiate issues and the personal were all addressed.

Conclusion

Finally, I would like to argue that part of a teacher's role in dealing with stress in teaching might be to argue for a co-ordinated and integrated picture of support at the institutional, classroom and individual level. In times of pressure this may not be well received, for the short-term strategy is often the one that is favoured. However, only a co-ordinated and serious approach to teacher stress will tackle an issue that is not going to go away and which needs to be taken more seriously than it is at the moment.

References

Cooper, C. and Travers, C. (1990), *Survey on Occupational Stress Among Teachers in the United Kingdom*, UMIST/NASUWT.

Cox, T., Boot, T. and Cox, S. (1989), 'Stress in Schools: A Problem-solving Approach', in M. Cole and S. Walker (eds), *Teaching and Stress*, Open University Press.

Cox, T. (1990), *Teachers and Schools: A Study of Organisational Health*, NUT.

DES (1989), *Discipline in Schools: (The Elton Report)*, HMSO.

Drummond, M.J. and McLaughlin, C. (1994) 'Teaching and Learning: The Fourth Dimension', in H. Bradley, G. Southworth and C. Connor (1994), *Developing Teachers, Developing Schools*, David Fulton Publishers.

Dunham, J. (1989), 'Personal, Interpersonal and Organizational Resources for Coping with Stress in Teaching', in M. Cole and S. Walker (eds), *Teaching and Stress*, Open University Press.

Esteve, J. (1989) 'Teacher Burnout and Teacher Stress', in M. Cole and S. Walker (eds), *Teaching and Stress*, Open University Press.

Johnstone, M. (1993), *Teachers' Workload and Associated Stress*, Scottish Council for Research in Education.

Kyriacou, C. (1989), 'The Nature and Prevalence of Teacher Stress', in M. Cole and S. Walker (eds), *Teaching and Stress*, Open University Press.

Kyriacou, C. and Sutcliffe, J. (1978) 'Teacher Stress: A Review', *Educational Studies* **4**.

Lodge, C., McLaughlin, C. and Best, R. (1992), 'Organizing Pastoral Support for Teachers: Some Comments and a Model', *Pastoral Care in Education,* June 1992.

McIntyre, T.C. (1984), 'The Relationship Between Locus of Control and Teacher Burnout', *British Journal of Educational Psychology* **54**.

NUT (1990), 'The Stress Factor', *The Teacher,* Spring 1990.

Rogers, W. (1996), *Managing Teacher Stress*, Pitman.

Smail, D. (1996), *How to Survive Without Psychotherapy*, Constable.

Woods, P. (1989), 'Stress and the Social Context', in M. Cole and S. Walker (eds), *Teaching and Stress*, Open University Press.

Index

■ ■ ■